TRAGIC PSALMS

Francis Patrick Sullivan

The Pastoral Press
Washington, DC

ACKNOWLEDGMENTS

The Bible Today   Jonah: An Oratorio
New Catholic World Psalms 137, 139

Book design and cover design
by Aileen Callahan

ISBN 0-912405-35-X

The Pastoral Press
225 Sheridan Street, NW, Washington, DC 20011
(202) 723-1254

The Pastoral Press is the publications division of the National Association of
Pastoral Musicians, a membership organization of musicians and clergy
dedicated to fostering the art of musical liturgy.

Drawings by Aileen Callahan
© 1987 by Aileen Callahan

CONTENTS

DRAWINGS BY AILEEN CALLAHAN

FOR MARGARET

FOR JEREMIAH
(+ 1983)

Introduction

The translations of psalms I offer here are in the
language of dramatic poetry, as contemporary as I can
make it. I explain at the end why I call them tragic.
After that I have put a libretto based on the Book of
Jonah. I hope by it to show how a tradition can
interpret itself. The explanation of the libretto becomes
a further reflection on the nature of the psalms
contained here. The work of Mitchell Dahood, of Carroll
Stuhlmueller, of Bonaventure Zerr, have served as the
basis for my study of these psalms. My gratitude to them
is great. The poetry of William Everson, of Frank Bidart,
of Richard Murphy has kept me aware of the vividness I
needed in language for dramatic translations. The
courage and skill of Burton Raffel as a translator has
been like a guiding spirit to me in the overall work of
doing these psalms as well as the ones in the lyric
volume. My gratitude to them is great. Again the
MacDowell Colony gave me a residency during which I
did most of the volume. I thank the Colony very much.
Aileen Callahan has again designed the book and graced
it with her own art. I thank her also and deeply, for this
and for other creations of hers for the way they stand in
their own light. I am grateful to composers who have set
to music some of the Lyric Psalms, and may set some of
these, Kevin Waters, David Haas, Michael Joncas, David
Gallagher, Laetitia Blain, Christopher Willcock. I love the
story of the stone soup. I have the pot, the water, the
stone, the fire. The ingredients arrive from all over.

PSALM 2

To rebel against God
    and against God's king
is stupid, so why do
    people call up troops,
and petty kings revolt,
    and clans concoct war:
"Break our bondage to them,
    get rid of the yoke!"
God mocks them from above,
    plays with their armies,
then in fury forces
    them to flee the field.
God anointed me king
    on Holy Sion.
Let me read aloud what
    God decreed for me:
"You are my son this day.
    I am your father.
Ask me for a kingdom
    and you shall have it,
nations for your subjects,
    the world for your wealth.
You will break their spirits
    with an iron rule,
break them like pottery."
    Come to your senses,
you rulers of this world!
    You have now been warned.
Treat God with due respect.
    And fear for your lives,
you are mortal beings.
    If you anger God,

and God angers quickly,
   your people perish.
But for those who trust God,
   life is a rich thing.

PSALM 3

God, they are many,
    many against me,
many on the rise
    who look to kill me!
"God will not save him!"
    they say, but you, God,
are my defender
    every day I live,
my majestic God.
    You give me courage.
One appeal from me
    and you respond from
your holy mountain.
    I do not fear sleep.
You keep me alive.
    I will wake for sure.
Nor do I fear shots
    people take at me
from every quarter.
    Come, save me, O God
my God, smash their mouths
    shut, smash their teeth in,
the whole wicked crowd.
    Be our salvation,
O God, be our grace!

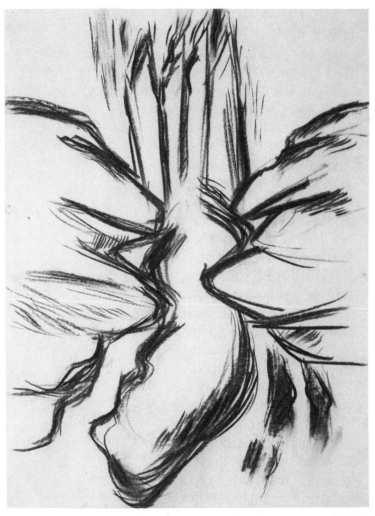

Psalm 5

PSALM 5

Hear what I say, O God,
   what I ask of you,
it is a cry for help
   to my God, my king,
it is a cry to you!
   Hear me when you dawn,
hear me plead when you rise,
   I will watch for you!
A god who is nothing
   hosts evil. Not you!
You never host evil!
   Let the arrogant
never approach your bench.
   I hate false worship.
Wipe out the blasphemy.
   You hate those people
whose gods are figurines.
   Your great love brings me
into your house to pray.
   I will worship you
in your holy Temple,
   O God, among those
who hold you in respect.
   Take me away from
my accusers into
   your peaceful pastures,
smooth my way before me.
   Their mouths are corrupt,
they stomach evil well,
   their throats are grave sites,
their tongues diggers of graves.
   Put a stop to them,

O God, with their own schemes.
  Pitch them down to death
for the multiple crimes
  they pitched in your face.
But those who want to stay
  with you will rejoice,
will sing a lasting song.
  You will protect them
so they love what you are.
  Their joy will be you.
And, O God, you will bless
  those who lead good lives,
your care will be their shield!

PSALM 7

O God, I put myself
  in your hands for safety.
I am under attack.
  Reach me before he does,
the lion who pounces,
  breaks the neck of its kill.
I have no help but you!
  O God, my God, if it
is true that I have fouled
  myself with idolatry,
that I have guilty palms,
  that I betrayed a friend,
hurt him with heedless talk,
  then let that lion catch
and kill me and drag my
  guts into hell and leave
my carcass there to rot.
  O God, let your anger
rise against the demonic
  pride of my enemies.
You be the judge yourself,
  O God, set up a court,
fill it with the nations,
  put them all on trial
and render a verdict!
  Be the judge of them all!
Judge me on my merits
  also, O God, judge me
on the way I have lived.
  Get back at treachery
and those who commit it.
  Encourage the just life

for you are a just God.
You see hidden motives.
God above, I am in
your hands, you, the Savior
of those who lead good lives.
Yours is a rule of law.
You make justice triumph.
I wish you would sharpen
your sword, I wish you would
draw a bead with your bow,
I wish you would get your
deadly weapons ready
to shoot flaming arrows.
Malice is like a seed
in the one who hates me,
evil like gestation,
treachery like a birth.
Trap him in his own trap.
Pitch him down his own hole.
Crown him with his own crime,
let it crack his own skull.
I will give you due thanks
for your justice to me,
O God above, and chant
the praises of your name.

PSALM 9

O God, I will have you
    to thank and thank fiercely
if my enemies run,
    ruined by your fury.
I will tell it abroad,
    the way you dealt with them.
I will take a savage
    joy in you, I will chant
your name, almighty God.
    I ask you to defend
me, O God of justice,
    in a cause that is right,
and to sit in judgment.
    Condemn heathen nations!
Destroy wicked peoples!
    Let no trace of them last!
Forget them forever!
    Murder my enemies,
make them lasting rubble,
    eradicate their gods,
out of sight, out of mind!
    You have reigned forever
from a throne of judgment.
    Your rule is a just rule
and fair for everyone.
    You defend the helpless,
defend them from danger.
    So we are to trust you,
those of us who love you.
    It is said you never
leave your own derelict.
    We are to chant your name,
God, the king of Sion,
    and tell the world your tale,

how you comfort people
    who are stricken with grief,
how you hear their keening,
    how you never forget
the sound of suffering.
    Feel what I feel, O God,
see the fear I live in
    from my enemy Death.
Take me off its threshold
    so I can say how good
you are from the threshold
    of your daughter Sion,
and boast of your triumph.
    Mire them in their own mud,
the ones who dug the pit.
    Snare them in their own snare,
the ones who rigged the net.
    May your judgments reveal
to the world what you are.
    Let those who commit crime
be captured red-handed
    and thrown back into hell.
And those who deny you,
    let them also perish.
The helpless are not doomed
    to final frustration,
and the oppressed not doomed
    to final loss of hope.
Stand up for us, O God,
    or the wicked will win.
Summon heathen nations
    before your tribunal.
Let them know how mortal
    they all are next to you!

PSALM 10

Why are you not with us
  when we suffer, O God,
why hide yourself away?
  There is evil brewing
in the criminal's heart.
  They are out after loot
so hard they cannot breathe.
  They brag about their schemes.
The crook loves crookedness
  and calls God a zero:
"God's rage is impotent.
  God will not interfere.
Money will always talk."
  Your law does not touch them,
O God, they disdain it.
  Each of them says: "No one
catches me! Life without
  a hitch or a bad day!"
Each of them spews curses
  and lies and viciousness.
Their tongues are pure evil.
  They work where there are crowds.
They lure the innocent
  to their ruination.
They spot helpless victims.
  No one knows a lion
is lurking in ambush
  to pounce on the weakest,
fang them and drag them off!
  They harry their victims
into nets, into pits.
  They mutter: "God forgets,

looks away, sees nothing."
Must the criminal type
get away with saying:
"God cannot punish us!"
And you let it happen,
the grief, the misery.
Come suffer it yourself!
You are the last resort
for the helpless victim.
Do anything you can.
Smash the power of crime.
Punish the criminal.
Are they so hard to spot?
Your rule is limitless.
Get rid of the culprits.
Listen to suffering,
O God, focus on it,
understand what it is.
Once you are on the side
of the helpless victim,
the arrogance of crime
will lose its power to
drive people to despair.

PSALM 11

I take shelter in God.
  So why try to kill me,
why hunt me like a bird?
  Yet you do, brace your bows,
fit arrows to the strings
  to let fly from ambush
at those who lead good lives!
  What does God make of it
when lives are demolished,
  the God who is enthroned
on earth in the temple
  as well as in the sky?
God sees and God judges
  what human beings do.
God is justice itself
  and will weigh wickedness.
Love of crime means hatred
  of life in anyone.
God send the wicked a
  hail of fire and brimstone,
a wind to scorch their lives.
  God is justice itself
and loves to see it done.
  This is the holy God
we will see face to face!

Psalm 12

PSALM 12

No one speaks the truth
    anymore, the people
who did are long gone.
    O God, will you help us!
Everybody lies
    to everybody else!
They lie in their teeth,
    they have double standards.
God cut their tongues out
    and the lies out with them!
They brag about it:
    "Lies make us powerful!
Lies are like weapons!
    No one can stop us!"
God gives them the lie:
    "I will make them stop it.
The poor are in tears,
    the helpless are groaning.
They will have from me
    all the help they cry for!"
There is no dross in
    the promises God makes.
They are like silver
    made molten and made pure,
or like potter's clay
    refined the seventh time.
You have guarded us,
    O God, eternal God,
from the very start.
    Liars lurk everywhere!
They dig us our grave!

Psalm 17

PSALM 17

I beg you for justice,
   O God, hear me out!
What I say is the truth.
   Destroy the liars!
Let me present my side,
   I am innocent.
I want you to see it.
   Look at my motives,
look at my hidden life,
   test me in the fire.
You will detect in me
   no use for idols.
I have never prayed to
   one of your creatures.
I kept your rule not to.
   I walked the hard road.
I never left the track.
   O God, I beg you,
heed my call for justice,
   listen to my case,
accept my argument!
   Kill those who curse you!
Stop the mouths of those who
   attack you, O God!
Keep me as you would keep
   the light of your eye,
be a shelter for me,
   the shadow of wings,
from the wicked fury
   that wants to tear me,
from the death-dealing kind
   circling around me.

They are bloated with pride.
They spout arrogance.
The time I showed weakness,
    they swarmed around me
with the look in their eyes
    to pitch me to hell,
they were like young lions
    crouching in ambush
eager to make the kill.
They are the wicked
who wage their war on you!
    Rescue me from them!
O God, kill them yourself,
    wipe them from the earth,
let them live no longer!
    But let the people
you prize fill their bellies.
    Let their children have
the joy of abundance.
    Let them hand it on
to their children to come.
    My joy will be to
see your face when I am
    proven innocent.
When I am free of Death,
    I will fill myself
with the glory you are!

Psalm 18

PSALM 18

You are my strength, O God,
  I am fierce for you,
my rock, my fort, my God,
  my route of escape,
my mountain hideaway,
  shield, power, safety,
bastion, boast of my life.
  I begged you to help
and you saved me from Death.
  Its waves broke on me,
a monstrous surf gripped me
  like a winding sheet.
I saw the gulf of Death.
  Panic made me pray,
pray you to rescue me.
  I reached you above,
my panic reached your ears.
  Hell shivered and shook,
the roots of the mountains,
  they all staggered drunk
when your wrath erupted.
  Your breath was a plume
of smoke, your mouth a flow
  of voracious fire,
and flecks of it shot out!
  You parted the air,
came down on a storm cloud,
  horsed on a cherub,
riding its stretch of wings.
  You brought a black pall
like a billowing tent.
  With whips of lightning,

(over)

you drove clouds before you,
  hurled hailstones and fire.
You boomed across the sky,
  an almighty voice,
shot flashes of lightning
  that struck all over.
One gust from you, O God,
  one mighty bellow,
and the sea was laid bare
  to its lowest depths
and the earth to its rock.
  You reached and grabbed me
right out of the water,
  you grabbed me from Death,
overmastering Death.
  On that deadly day,
your strength marched before me
  through that deadly place.
You brought me out alive.
  You wanted me free
because I kept your law,
  this was your reward.
I have always kept it.
  I have never sinned
against you, O my God.
  I study your law,
study it constantly.
  My motives are clear,
my behavior careful,
  not to offend you.
And you rewarded me
  for the life I led

because my hands were clean,
    by your own judgment.
If we keep faith, you do,
    if we are honest,
you are, and if sincere,
    then you are with us,
but if we deceive you,
    then you deceive us.
Your power saves the poor,
    almighty power,
but the proud you dismiss
    with their haughty looks.
You are the lamp that lights
    my darkness, O God.
I can run strong in you.
    With you as my God,
I can take any wall.
    Your rule is total.
Your word is well tested.
    Your power defends
all those who trust in you.
    Who else is like you,
like the mountain you are?
    You gave me my strength,
you, the ruler of all,
    made me sure-footed
like deer who stand on crags.
    You taught me to fight,
gave me your special bow,
    your triumphant shield,
your right hand to hold me.
    You won the battle.

(over)

You made me look superb,
   gave me a great stride
and legs to bear the strain.
   I caught those who fled,
kept after them until
   there was not one left.
I struck them, down they went,
   at my feet, to stay.
You gave me battle strength.
   You cut down my foes,
they fell beneath my feet,
   I stood on their necks,
I decimated them.
   They begged you for help,
but you abandoned them,
   you, almighty God,
you answered them nothing.
   I ground them to dust
underfoot, I squashed them
   like mud in the streets.
You deflected the shots
   my enemies took,
you protected me from
   their lethal intent.
They are now my subjects,
   these foreign peoples.
One word and they obey.
   They cringe like cowards,
they wither before me,
   the heart out of them.
Be my God forever!
   Let the world praise you,

God, my mountain of strength.
    Let the world prize you,
God, my source of triumph.
    You won my battle,
gave me conquered nations,
    kept me free of Death,
free of all attackers,
    of all backbiters!
I will sing your praises,
    God, throughout the world,
and make your name famous.
    You made me well known
as a conquering king.
    You took care of me
as you cared for David,
    your anointed one,
and his line forever!

PSALM 20

God give you the battle!
Jacob's God defend you!
Send you help from Sion,
help from the holy heights!
God keep your gifts in mind,
your generous cattle!
God give you what you want!
Success to all your plans!
So we may boast your win
and hold our banners high
to honor our God's name!
God give you all you ask!

It comes to me that God
gives the king the battle!
From the height of heaven
comes the gift of triumph.
From the fortress above
comes the might that wins.
We are strong in God's name,
not in our chariots
and not in our horses,
as our enemies are.
They have come tumbling down
while we stood tall and strong!
The battle went to the king
when we asked it of God!

PSALM 21

The king is ecstatic,
  God, you won his battle,
it is what he wanted
  and what he begged you for;
it is what you gave him.
  And you gave him a ripe
future and a crown of gold.
  You gave him endless days
just as he had asked you,
  days, lasting, lasting days!
He glows with the glory
  of your triumph in war,
a majestic figure!
  Your gifts will never cease.
You will give him yourself
  to behold forever.
The king depends on you,
  his loyalty is firm.
You took the enemy,
  left hand, right hand, you took
all those who hated you
  and you pitched them into
a fiery furnace,
  O God, you swallowed them
live, you ate them with fire!
  You rooted out their race
to the last child they had.
  They plotted rebellion.
It was a wicked scheme.
  It was doomed to failure.
You aimed at them point blank,
  they cowered before you.

(over)

Glory in your triumph,
   O God, and we will shout
our praise to your power!

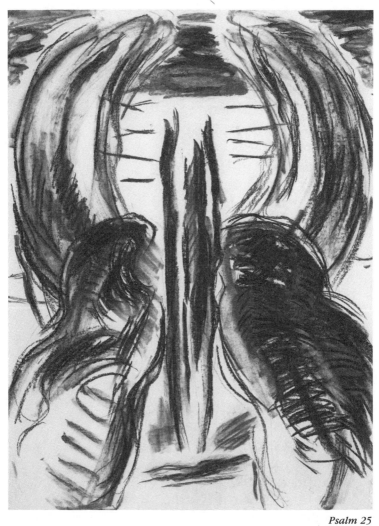

Psalm 25

PSALM 25

I look to you, God,
   to you the one I trust,
let me not be fooled,
   let no one laugh at me!
You never make fools
   of those who pray to you.
The fools are the ones
   who make empty speeches.
You are the teacher
   I want, O God, and yours
are the ways I want.
   Teach me to follow you
faithfully for
   you are what will save me!
You are the one I
   pray to, day in, day out!
God, stay mindful of
   your age old compassion,
your age old kindness,
   and not the rebel life
I led in my youth,
   and when you think of me,
keep to your kindness,
   keep to your loving ways.
The justice God is
   is the justice God shows
to sinful people,
   the justice God uses
to guide the gentle,
   to teach the poor to live.
The ways of kindness
   and truth are ways of God

for those who obey.
  To be true to yourself,
forgive me my sins,
  I know they are many.
If you respect God,
  God will guide your choices.
Your life will go well,
  your children own the land.
You can be God's friend
  if you respect the law
God reveals to friends.
  I look only to God
to free me from sin.
  Take notice of me, God,
be compassionate,
  I am hurt and alone.
I am sore with grief.
  Take me away from this.
Look at how my sins
  trouble me and lift them.
Look at the number
  of enemies I have,
treacherous people.
  Give me an honesty,
an integrity,
  to guard me when I pray.
And free Israel
  from her troubles, God!

PSALM 28

I plead for my life,
    O God, my strength.
If you stay silent
    and do nothing,
I am dead and gone.
    Please spare my life.
I ask this of you
    with hands lifted
towards your holy place.
    Do not lump me
with wicked people,
    with criminals.
They talk peace abroad,
    but plan for war.
Pay them back in kind!
    Treachery for
treachery is right!
    And for the crimes
they commit, give them
    their just deserts!
They have no respect
    for God's power,
nor God's creation.
    God will make them
a heap of rubble
    and leave them there.
My thanks to you, God!
    You saved my life.
You protected me.
    I knew you would.
I can live again.
    My joy is full.

It will be my song
    of thanks to you.
You keep us from harm.
    You save our king.
Keep our people free.
    Bless what you prize.
Guide us like a flock
    and carry us
with you forever!

Psalm 35

PSALM 35

Battle those who battle
   me! Battle them, O God!
Buckle on your armor
   and be ready to fight!
Have your weapons at hand
   and keep the hounds at bay.
People want to kill me.
   Make them a mockery,
baffle them totally
   in their plots to harm me.
Whip them away like chaff
   a deadly wind chases
into the murk of death,
   a deadly wind from God.
They laid a trap for me,
   set a net to catch me,
they watched my every move.
   Let the trap spring on them,
and the net tie them tight.
   Let them end up in knots!
My joy will be in God,
   in God winning for me.
My whole soul will cry out
   "No one is like you, God!
You free oppressed people
   who cannot free themselves.
You free the poor and pained
   from those who prey on them."
I must face false witness,
   must answer false questions.
Goodness invites evil.
   That cuts me to the quick!

(over)

While they led the good life,
    I wore a sackcloth robe.
I fasted severely,
    I hugged my life of prayer
like a friend, a brother.
    I was like a mourner
who had lost a mother,
    somber and stooped in grief.
If I made a mistake,
    I drew a mocking crowd
eager to harass me.
    Not a one did I know!
And they did harass me
    and had no mind to stop!
A ring of gnashing teeth!
    How long will it last, Lord,
and you just stand and watch!
    Keep me free of their traps,
free of their lionish teeth!
    I will give public thanks
to you when the people
    throng together for prayer.
Do not let those liars
    turn me into a joke
with their wink of the eye.
    They have no thought of peace,
they batten on the poor.
    They scheme, and wickedly,
against me, mouths agape:
    "Ha! We can hit him now!"
Do not stay aloof, God,
    do not keep your distance.

Free me, fight for me,
    take on my struggle, God,
your own sense of justice
    calls you to my defense.
O God, let them not win
    or they will brag of it:
"Ha! We ate him up! Ha!
    We swallowed him alive!"
Make them a mockery,
    who boast of beating me.
Shroud them in utter shame.
    They lie to wreck my life!
Let there be joy for those
    who want to see me saved,
so they can say from then on:
    "It is a mighty God
who wants to keep us safe!"
    I will add my own praise
of your justice to theirs
    as long as the days last!

Psalm 36

PSALM 36

A false god works
   in wicked people.
   They have lost all fear
of the true God,
   who will destroy them
   once their sin is known.
   One look will do it.
They are liars,
   every word they say.
   They are too much brute
to live by truth.
   Asleep or awake,
   they worship false gods.
They live for them,
   never miss a chance
   to do what is wrong.
Your love, O God,
   comes pure as the sky.
Your faith, O God,
   comes pure as the clouds.
Your gift of self,
   grand as mountain peaks.
Your care for us,
   a bottomless sea.
   All things grow in you,
   men, women, and beasts.
A precious care,
   O God. All creatures,
   men, women, and gods,
find safety in
   the shadow you cast.
   They live off the fat

(over)

of your household,
  they drink the delights
of your richness
  streaming before them.
Life springs from you,
  and light we see by
  in your lasting field.
Keep your love strong
  for those who know you
  as the only God.
Stay generous
  to those who stay good.
Let not the lie
  of idolatry
  catch me unawares.
Let evil not
  knock me off my feet.
See how they fall,
  those who love false gods.
Once they are down,
  they can never rise.

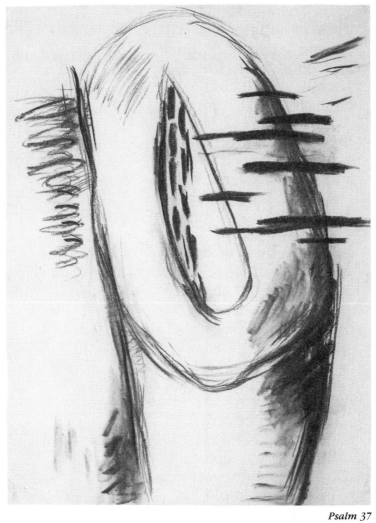

Psalm 37

PSALM 37

Stay cool about crime
   and criminals.
They perish like grass,
   soon green, soon gone.
Stay good and with God,
   close to the land,
feed off its rich crops.
   Your heart is home
if your joy is God.
   Give God your life
and see God shape it,
   make it holy,
make it pure as light;
   see its justice
shine bright as noon.
   So let God work.
Stay cool about those
   who amass wealth
by fraudulent deals
   they carry off.
No anger, no rage,
   no loss of peace
that harms only you.
   God will cut down
all criminal types,
   but God will give
the land to those who pray.
   In a short time
the wicked perish.
   Look in the door!
No one to be found!
   But the gentle,

the land becomes theirs,
   theirs the delight
in the earth's rich crops!
   So the wicked
want to do them in,
   hot with hatred.
But God will laugh last.
   God sees their death,
draw what swords they want,
   shoot what arrows,
to kill what paupers
   or derelicts,
to murder people
   who lead good lives.
They die by the sword
   themselves, their bows
are broken to bits.
   It is better
to be poor and good
   than rich and bad.
For the rich and bad
   will be broken,
but God will shelter
   the poor and good.
As for honest wealth,
   God protects it,
guarantees that it
   will last and last.
The honest will not
   wither from drought;
they will have plenty
   come famine time,

(over)

not wither away.
    The bad shrivel,
they get tinder dry
    and burn like brush
in waterless draws
    and they vanish
quicker than the smoke.
    The bad borrow
but never repay.
    What the good give,
they give from the heart.
    The land is theirs,
they are blessed by God.
    The bad are cursed
by God and cut down.
    God makes the good
stride a steady road,
    and if they trip,
God still holds them fast.
    They do not fall.
I have never seen
    the good go bare,
their children beg, and
    I have lived long.
They give without stint,
    thus their children
share in their reward.
    If you want life
that lasts, then be just,
    give up evil.
God never deserts
    those who keep faith,

but kills the wicked
   to the last child.
The good get the land
   to have and hold.
They never lose it.
   They speak the truth,
they say what is just,
   they live the law
of God from the heart.
   They do not sin.
When the sinful plot
   to kill the just,
God prevents the plot.
   And if the just
are falsely accused,
   God will not let
them be found guilty.
   Let God be God
and obey the law,
   and you will grow
to own the land whole.
   And when the bad
are cut down by God,
   you will know joy.
The bad can stand tall,
   I have seen them,
stand lush as a tree
   on fertile soil.
But they were soon dead
   and left no trace.
I looked. Nothing there!
   Integrity

(over)

will give you long life,
  and honesty,
use them as your guides.
  Perversity
will give you short life,
  and wickedness
wipe away what's left.
  Those who love God
will be safe in God,
  in a fortress
when evil attacks.
  God is the one
to save them, the one
  to rescue them,
God is the one to
  keep them from harm
when they ask God's help,
  God is the one!

PSALM 41

They are a gift of God,
   people who guard their tongues.
God keep them from danger,
   protect, prolong their lives,
enrich their days on earth,
   save them from hungry death.
If sickness lays them low,
   may God look after them
and nurse them back to health,
   and stand them on their own.
I prayed: "O God, hear me,
   heal me in spite of sin
committed against you."
   There are those who hate me,
who want the opposite:
   "Is it not time he died?
Time his name was nothing?"
   And those who visit me
say what they do not mean!
   They see only the worst,
then they spread the bad news,
   a whispering campaign.
They are dead set, O God!
   They mean to do me in!
"Slip him a poisoned drink
   so he never gets up!"
I even had a friend
   tell lies behind my back,
a friend I fed at home.
   God hear me, God heal me,
so I may harm them back!
   I will know you love me

(over)

if they do not down me!
  I have kept faith with you.
Lift me into your life,
  keep me there forever.
O God of Israel,
  may the thanks we offer
you never, never stop!

PSALM 44

O God, we took as true
  what our tradition taught!
You did things in the past
  to save your people's life.
You rooted others up,
  you put us in their place.
You weeded others out
  to give us room to grow.
No sword could win that land,
  no military might.
Your power alone could,
  the flash of your fury
for the people you loved.
  You are King, God, Leader!
You are Jacob's Savior!
  On the strength of your name
we broke our enemies,
  we walked right over them,
no need to trust the bow,
  nor trust the sword to win,
you were enough for us
  to rout them in disgrace.
You were our boast back then.
  We had nothing but praise!
Then you left us naked.
  You deserted our ranks.
You left us, cut and run,
  left us behind like loot
for the enemy's lust,
  or sheep marked for the kill,
or lost like refugees.
  You got next to nothing

(over)

for us, you sold us cheap,
   made us a mockery
to neighboring peoples,
   a laugh, a bitter joke,
something ridiculous
   to everyone's delight.
It is utter disgrace.
   I stand before myself
like someone stripped and shamed
   when I hear their voices
taking revenge on me,
   the catcalls, the curses.
The shame is absolute!
   We do not deserve it!
We kept our word to you!
   We kept our hearts loyal!
We kept our ways straight!
   You brought total chaos
down on us like darkness.
   If we had forgotten
you were God, if we had
   prayed to an alien god,
you would have found it out,
   would have spotted the lie.
The reason we suffer
   is not that! It is you!
We are marked for the kill
   like sheep for you non-stop!
Are you aware of it,
   O Lord, are you aware?
Is your anger so blind?
   Have you forgotten why

we are tortured and torn?
   We are face down in death,
flat as a bunch of stiffs!
   Wake up to what goes on!
Get us out of this for
   the love you say you are!

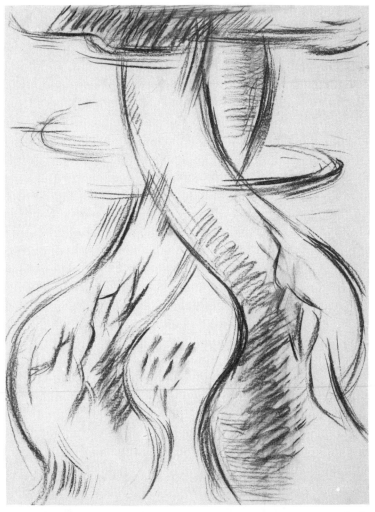

Psalm 45

PSALM 45

I have a marriage song
   to sing for you, my Lord.
May my lyrics be clear
   as the stroke of a pen.
You were gifted by God
   before the dawn of time,
the fairest of the fair,
   the kindest of the kind.
Strap your sword to your hip
   and hold the world in hand
by your majestic strength.
   Win the day for the truth,
take the side of the poor.
   May your battle for them
and the weapons you wield
   make you known to the world,
so nations surrender,
   foolish to fend you off!
God, the everlasting,
   has placed you on your throne.
Justice is the scepter
   by which you are to rule.
Justice, what you must love,
   evil, what you must hate.
You have been marked by God.
   You breathe the balm of joy,
your clothes have the rich scent
   of myrrh, aloes, and balsam.
Your halls are ivory,
   your people a pleasure,
your courtiers royal,
   the daughters of rulers.

(over)

And the Queen at your side
　robed in golden Ophir.
O daughter, heed my voice:
　Forget your kith and kin.
Your beauty draws the king.
　Now he is Lord for you.
You owe him your respect.
　The purple robe is yours.
The feast longs to see you.
　Your dress is royal dress,
entirely lined with gold,
　woven by the women
who work with golden thread.
　Lead the bride to the king,
have her women follow,
　all with jubilation,
to the royal palace!
　Replace your parentage
with children of your own,
　create a royal line!
I sing for you, my Lord,
　to spread your name abroad,
to have the world praise you,
　as long as time will last!

Psalm 46

PSALM 46

We have God
   from long ago
      as our defense
against Death,
   a proven God!
We need not fear
   even hellmouth,
      even mountains
picked up and pitched
   into the sea,
      the sea of Death!
Let it roar,
   let it seethe,
      let it cough
the mountains up,
   let it stand
      the river
         on its head
in its channel!
   God is the joy
      of the city
God makes sacred.
   She is safe
   with her God
   at her heart
who will help her
   at the dawn
      of battle
         at daybreak.
People quiver,
   nations quake,
      at the thunder

of God's voice.
    They back away.
Our mighty God
    is Jacob's God,
        is our defense.
See how God
    makes the earth
        bring forth fruit,
wins all wars
    on the earth
        end to end,
snaps the bow,
    breaks the spear,
        burns the shield,
says to us:
    "Stay with me.
    I am God.
I hold power
    over the world
        and its peoples."
We have God,
    Jacob's God,
        almighty God,
            as our defense!

Psalm 47

PSALM 47

Applaud and cheer,
  with all your might,
    a greater God,
      you little gods,
Our splendid God,
  King of the world!
God made nations
  bow before us,
    fall at our feet!
God made our realm
  a special realm,
    Jacob's people
  a special love.
Hurrah! Hurrah!
  God's procession
    ascends the mount,
let trumpets sound!
  Shout praise, shout praise,
    you little gods,
  shout praise, shout praise
to God our King!
  King of the earth,
    O little gods,
      sing your song well!
  King of nations,
throned above them!
  All you princes,
    stand together
      around the throne!
Abraham's God
  is the strongest,
    and rules you all!
Almighty God!

Psalm 48

PSALM 48

Praised be God's might!

Inside our city
   is God's holy mountain,
a thing of beauty,
   a joy to the whole world.
Sion is God's home,
   the heart of God's city.
God is her fortress,
   God is her battlement.
Once kings joined forces
   for a massive assault.
One look at Sion
   made them stop in panic,
ready to desert,
   then fear took hold of them,
pain contorted them
   like women in labor,
like Tyrian ships
   shattered by gale force winds.
We see the story
   come true in the city
of Almighty God,
   she is safe forever!
Here, in your Temple,
   God, we relish your care.
There, under your sky,
   God, the earth fills with praise.
You are generous.
   Sion and the cities
of Judah should dance
   over the gifts you give.

(over)

Circle the city
    and tote up her towers,
and inspect her walls,
    and note her battlements,
then tell your offspring:
    "God has made this city!"
God everlasting,
    and our eternal guide.

PSALM 49

Mark me, mark me well,
  everyone, everywhere,
no matter your birth,
  no matter your riches.
You must hear the truth.
  It is a hard-earned truth
about life and death
  to the stroke of my harp:
Why envy the rich?
  Even on your deathbed,
even surrounded
  by malicious watchers
who think wealth will save
  them, superior wealth?
No one owns this life.
  It is not bought from God.
Death has all the cash
  and down they go for good.
No one buys heaven,
  no one skips out on Death.
If God bats an eye,
  the wise, the foolish, drop
and leave others rich.
  Forever is the grave.
There they stay for good
  though their names above ground
still mark the estates.
  Death is the sleep of sleeps.
They vanish like beasts.
  It is final for them,
the rich, the pampered.
  Death will herd its flock

(over)

down into the Pit,
   and the maw of the Pit,
the hungry maw, will
   swallow them like cattle.
But God will save me,
   pull me from Death's clutches.
Feel no envy for
   the ones who grow wealthy
and have rich estates.
   They take nothing with them
when they go below,
   though they were lords of life.
And praised though you be
   for your wealth, once you die,
you blend with the dead
   who never see the sun.
The rich, the pampered,
   they never see the truth.
They just stop, like beasts!

PSALM 52

You champ hypocrite!
 Why brag devotion
  and bring destruction
as if God wants it!
 You evil cocoon!
 You razor sharp tongue!
 You master liar!
You love in reverse,
 evil over good,
  lies over the truth.
You relish all the
 harm your tongue can cause.
May God stamp you out
 for good, seed and all,
whip your life away,
 whip your children too!
This will be fearful
 at first for the just,
  but turn to laughter:
"So he did not need
 a God to help him!
 He had his money.
 He had his power
to lean on. So look!"
 I choose to be like
the olive tree in
 God's house, I will trust
myself to the love
 of the lasting God!
O lasting God, I
 thank you for acting.
I tell the world you
 are good to your own!

PSALM 53

They are stupid
  who do hideous things
  because there is no God,
there is no good.
Heaven watches
  every human being.
  God can see even one
who looks upward.
Not one of them
  is moral—all stupid
  apart, together all
corrupt—not one!
Can they ignore
  that they eat what belongs
  to God when they gorge on
God's own people!
They massed their troops
  but the siege failed because
  God made them skeletons.
You feared their bones.
So God stacked them.
  Let Sion bear new life.
Let God remake
  Israel, let Jacob
be fat with joy!

PSALM 54

Let your name, God,
let your power be my defense,
I plead with you!
O God, hear me!
Savage forces are on the march.
They are heathens. They want me dead.
But God guides me. They did not know.
They know it now, how God backed me,
Lord of my life, source of my strength.
God beat them at their own evil,
the savages,
turned them into total nothings,
my faithful God!
Generous God,
I offer you a gift in thanks.
I praise your name, God, your good name.
You saved me from savage forces.
I feasted my eyes
on their fall!

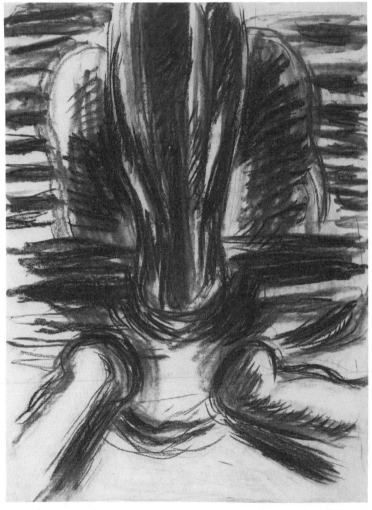

Psalm 55

PSALM 55

Hear me, heed me, God!
  Do not play ignorant!
Give me an answer.
  I need you in my grief!
I quake at hostile
  voices, at hate-filled stares.
They pile on curses.
  They smear me in public.
My heart loses count
  at the terror of death.
I shiver and shake
  when the terrors attack.
I need wings to fly
  out of here, like a bird,
fly far and be safe,
  out in the wilds somewhere.
I would whistle home,
  escape the wind, the storm.
God, destroy people
  who say things with forked tongues!
All I see is strife
  and crime in the city
at large night and day,
  and malice aforethought
policing its walls.
  Center city is crime,
  it is home to crime,
  it is fraud and force
  from its city soul.
It was friend, not foe,
  who buried me in slander,
not an enemy

(over)

to hide from who smeared me,
one of my own kind,
    close friend and confidant.
There was affection
    between us, in God's house,
we walked with the rest.
    But death to such people,
death alive in hell,
    for only poisonous words
leave their mouths, their minds.
    But I prayed and God heard,
morning noon and night
    I put my case to God.
God the redeemer
    heard me and saved my life.
God sided with me
    when others opposed me,
heard and heeded me,
    the God of Old answered,
whose ways never change.
    But no one stopped for fear.
My friend raised his hand
    against his closest friend,
broke the sacred bond;
    his words were smooth as silk,
were soothing as balm,
    but his mind was on war,
his words became swords.
    Our source of life is God,
the hand that feeds us,
    the one who never lets

justice stumble blind.
    O God, pitch the unjust
down to filthy death!
    Cut in half the lifespan
of idolaters!
    I want no part with them!
What I want is you!

Psalm 56

PSALM 56

The hunt is on, O God!
 For me! I need your help!
It is non-stop slander,
 tongues wagging at both ends!
 Vicious people hounding
 me every daylight hour!
I have to fight a mob!
When fear strikes me, O God
 I have you I can trust!
And you who tear at me,
 I will fling God at you,
 The God I can trust in,
 and then I fear no one!
You cannot get to me!
They poke at me non-stop,
 plot against me non-stop,
cook up surprise attacks!
 Look at those crooks watch me!
 Like thieves in the bushes!
Save us from their malice,
 O God, let loose your wrath,
 put down faithless nations!
Log my anguish yourself.
 List my tears on a page,
 my troubles on a scroll.
If they stop their attacks
 when I appeal to God,
 then God is on my side!
And you who tear at me,
 and you who tear at me,
I will fling God at you,
 I will fling God at you,

(over)

The God I can trust in,
   and then I fear no one!
You cannot get to me!
   I will keep faith in you,
     keep praising you, O God!
I ask you to free me
   from death, to steer me clear
of the road to nowhere.
   Let me walk in your sight
in fields that are alive!

Psalm 57

PSALM 57

Watch over me, God,
   watch over me,
hide my soul under
   the wings of night
till the threat is gone.
   To God above,
the Avenging God
   above, I pray.
God will send help down
   to get me free
of those who stalk me
   with their jeering,
love to sustain me,
   faith to keep me.
I move among men
   who are like beasts
but stalk human prey,
   their speech a spear,
an arrow, their tongue
   sharp as a sword.
You are beyond their
   reach, your beauty
broods over the earth.
   They rig a net
to trip me, a noose
   to hang me, they
dig a pit to pitch
   me on my face.
Let them fall in first!
   My love is strong,
God, my faith is strong,
   I will chant them.

Come alive my heart,
    alive my harp,
to make the dawn live.
    I will sing thanks
to you, God, though I
    be with pagans
in pagan places.
    Your love is large
as heaven, your faith
    large as the sky.
You are beyond our
    reach, your beauty
broods over the earth.

PSALM 58

You should be just
  in your verdicts
if you are leaders,
  if you are experts.
But no! You are not!
  You are malicious!
    You are capricious!
You dirty your hearts.
You dirty your hands.
  You were wicked and
    ugly from the start.
  You were born liars.
You are poisonous,
  like a bunch of snakes,
and deaf as a snake
  no charmer can charm,
no wizard handle.
  Defang them, O God,
knock their teeth out as
  you would lions' cubs.
Let them drop like falls,
  be weak as shadows
    when they fight a war,
rack them with disease
  so they die hard deaths,
or let them not live,
  be like the stillborn.
. . . .
  . . . .
But those who stay just
  will win and love it,

and wash off the blood
  of wicked judges.
And the world will say:
  Yes, the truth wins out!
Yes, there is a God
  who judges the judge!

PSALM 59

Fend for me, God!
   I have enemies.
Stand between us,
   they worship idols,
worship evil.
   Look at the ambush
they set for me.
   They are powerful
men who plot them.
   For no fault of mine,
for nothing, God,
   they are set to charge,
for no reason.
   Stand here when they do.
Watch them attack.
   God, mighty God, God
of Israel,
   come alive to them,
the pagan pack,
   the home-grown traitors,
show no mercy!
   They wait for the dark,
then like stray dogs
   they prowl the city.
They spew evil,
   words that cut like swords.
"There is no God!"
   But you laugh last, God!
You make them fools,
   the whole pagan pack.
God is my fort,
   I am more than safe.

God fends for me
　　like some battlement.
God clears my way,
　　I will defeat those
who malign me.
　　Kill them, God, and keep
us in courage,
　　send them reeling back
from your fortress
　　and ship them to hell!
God is our shield!
　　Trap them in their lies,
their wicked lies,
　　and rid us of them,
their arrogance,
　　curses and slander.
Get so angry
　　you finish them off,
you leave no one,
　　so they are nothing!
Then they might learn
　　that God rules the earth
from rim to rim.
　　They wait for the dark,
then like stray dogs
　　they prowl the city
growling for prey,
　　and if they find none
they growl the more.
　　But I chant your strength
in song each dawn.
　　I sing your power

(over)

to keep me safe
   when they attack me.
God is my fort,
   I am more than safe.
God fends for me
   Like some battlement!

PSALM 60

God, we provoked you,
  you stormed away.
You gave us your back
  in your anger.
You made the land quake,
  split it apart.
It swayed back and forth
  on its fractures.
You had us swallow
  to the dregs a
wine that made us sick.
  Give your faithful
a flag they can form
  around when the
arrows start flying.
  Use your power.
Make us win the war
  so the people
you love may be saved!

  The oracle
God spoke to us goes:
  "I will be glad
to make Shechem mine,
  to leave my mark
on Succoth Valley.
  Mine Gilead
and mine Manasseh.
  Ephraim my
helmet, Judah my
  battle baton.

(over)

Moab my wash bowl.
    I will trample
Edom underfoot.
    I will roar and
take Philistia."

    Who will capture
Petra for me, make
    me Edom's king?
And you, God, do you
    stay angry with
us and not campaign
    ever again
with our men at war?
    You be our help
against enemies.
    Human help is
futile against them.
    With you we win.
You will trample down
    those who face us.

Psalm 61

PSALM 61

This is a plea!
   Hear it, O God, hear it!
This is a plea
   from the brink of the grave.
   The heart is out of me.
Lead me above
   from here below to your
deathless mountain!
   Protect me from death.
   Be like a stone tower,
be like a tent
   to live in forever,
   a wing to hide beneath.
Listen to me,
   I am devoted to you,
Grant what I ask,
   I live my life for you.
Lengthen the life
   of your king; make his years
   become generations;
make his throne stand
   in your lasting presence;
and to flank him,
   love and fidelity.
I will thank you,
   and praise your name in song,
and live my life,
   day in, day out, for you!

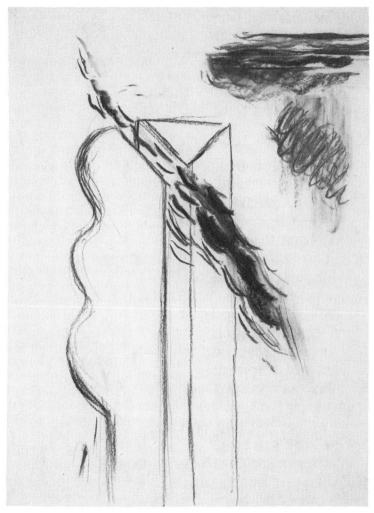

Psalm 62

PSALM 62

My base of strength
  is God and no one else.
My heart knows it.
  In God I will survive,
in God alone,
  my mountain, my fortress.
I am not trapped!

  Will you keep at a man
with bloated lies?
  You, like walls or fences
ready to croak!
  You think nothing but lies.
You love the kill.
  Your mouths are all blessing,
your hearts all curse!

  My solid hope is God,
my one mountain,
  one fortress, one triumph.
I am not trapped!.
  My survival is God,
glorious God,
  my rugged battlements,
God, my safety.
  Then trust God at all times.
Pour your hearts out,
  your solid hope is God.
Peasants are mist
  and princes a mirage,
lighter than leaves,
  and both lighter than breath!

Do not adore
   blackmail, do not adore
amassing wealth.
   And what God says, heed it!
And God has said
   two things for us to heed:
"All might is God's:
   God is unshakeable.
And all judgment:
   on each for what we do!"

Psalm 63

PSALM 63

This life makes me thirst
   for you, O God, my God.
My soul and body
   burn both with thirst for you
like drought-stricken fields
   that beg for rain to come.
I want to see you,
   your beauty and power,
in your holy place.
   The taste of your love is
richer to me than
   this life, this song, this praise!
So let me bless you,
   let me pray to you there
where life lasts for good,
   and there fill my hunger
with your food and drink,
   even as my joy spills out
to you in its thanks.
   Here, awake in my bed,
I think about you
   as I stare in the dark:
"If you would just help!
   Just give me a safe place!
Your shadow, your wings!
   I want to cling to you,
and you cling to me!"
   May the murdering kind
who want my life land
   in the bottom of hell!
May death cut them down
   with a double-edged sword,

(over)

fit food for jackals.
   But the king will glory
in God, and the rest
   of the faithful as well,
but those who speak lies
   will end up mute in death!

PSALM 64

I plead with you, God,
　　vicious liars hound me,
my life is at stake,
　　shield me from the malice
they concoct for me,
　　their tongues sharp as a knife,
　　poisoned as an arrow.
They shoot from ambush
　　at innocent people,
their lies quick and bold.
They intend to kill,
　　the poison is subtle.
"Who sees us?" they think.
　　"Lies are the perfect crime!"
God sees! The Searcher
　　of the soul within us,
the heart's twists and turns.
　　May God let fly at them,
pierce them through and through!
God will trip them in lies,
　　make them lick the dust.
We will all be affected.
　　And all tell the tale.
We will know what God did.
　　Those who do not lie
　　will take joy in God
　　and make God their shelter.
Let the innocent heart
　　be the glory of God.

PSALM 68

Let God show,
   the enemy scatters,
      cuts and runs,
driven away like smoke,
   gone like wax a flame licks.
Let God show,
   wickedness vanishes!
But the good,
   they go wild at the sight,
      sing and dance
and shout their ecstasy!

You spirits, you sky world,
   sing your songs,
cut a road through the clouds
   for God's ride,
hurrah! hurrah! for God!

From holy heights, God is
   parent for the orphan,
      shelter for the widow!
The God who gave nothings
   a country,
freed them singing from jail,
   and buried in the wastes
      their bull-headed jailers!

When you, O God, went out
   across the wilderness
      ahead of your people,
the ground shook, rain appeared,
   just at the sight of you,

God of Sinai,
God of Israel.

Gracious God,
  give us rain, abundant rain,
    bring law back to your land
and people,
  bring food for your faithful
  and rain to rescue them.

Let God speak,
  our battalions will shout,
their chiefs will surrender,
  armies and all give up,
    give up prize pastureland.
Let them leave it empty
  like sheep back in the fold.
We will be doves with gold
  feathers and silver wings.
God blanketed their chiefs
  as snow blankets Zalmon.

Mountainous, mountainous
  Bashan, you rugged range,
why envy one mountain,
  rugged range, one mountain?
God chose to make it home,
  make it home forever!

Thousands, invisible
  thousands, the chariots
of God, invisible

(over)

95

thousands of God's archers
made Sinai God's temple.
    You scaled its battlements,
took its forces captive,
    took the tribute they paid,
and buried chaotic
    forces, God, forever!
God be blessed,
    day in, day out, the God
        who took our pain away.
It is God,
    it is God who saved us,
        who got us free of death.
It is God
    who marched out of heaven,
God who struck
    the forces of chaos
        and split their skulls in two.
For God said:
    "I choked off the Dragon
        and shut tight the sea's mouth."
God waded through their blood,
    they were food for God's hounds.

Watch how God approaches,
    God, my king, approaches
        from the height of heaven,
choir first, musicians last,
    between them,
women beating small drums.
    Let God be blessed by all,
by Israel convoked!
    Watch young Benjamin lead,
        then the chiefs of Judah,

the chiefs of Zabulun,
the chiefs of Naphtali.

Be our strength, O God, be
the strength of what you built!
Jerusalem, it is
your holy place, it is
where kings will bring you gifts.
Smash crocodile Egypt
lurking in its reed swamp,
that stampede of wild beasts
who run amok for loot
over the backs of nations,
who love war, love riot!
Instead, have merchants bring
you blue cloth from Egypt,
have Cush bring you its wares.
O princes of the earth,
O princes of the sky,
sing, sing, to God, your praise!

Look at God ride the clouds
in the wilds of the sky.
Listen to the thunder,
the mighty voice of God,
the celestial God
of Israel, give praise!
whose glory, whose power
the sky cannot contain,
whose beauty overwhelms
the places that hold it,
but is Israel's God,
our courage, our conquest!
My people, praise your God!

PSALM 69

Will you save me, God!
   I am up to my neck
in Death, in its waters,
   its bottomless mud where
I sink without footing,
   its fathomless sea where
a suction pulls me down.
   I am weak with calling
and my voice has gone hoarse.
   My eyes play tricks on me,
O God, watching, waiting.
   There are more liars here
than I have hairs to count,
   and they lie about me
so often I lose track,
   as if I am the thief
and must restore the loot!
   You know I do foolish
things, God, my faults lie bare.
   May I not scandalize
people who look to you,
   God of power and might,
nor be a cause of shame
   to those who pray to you.
You are the reason why
   I am abused and shamed.
My brothers and sisters
   treat me as a stranger.
Those who hate you ravage
   me, make me the target
when they want to hit you.
   I got only abuse

when I fasted and prayed,
    and only mockery
in sackcloth and ashes,
    and revelers made me
the butt of drunken jokes.
    Yet I still pray to you,
God, be good to me now,
    be loving and save me,
be faithful, do not let
    me vanish in death's mud,
my enemy death, free
    me from its fathoms deep,
do not let its suction
    swallow me, nor its deeps,
nor hellmouth close its maw.
    Do as I beg you, God,
your love is generous.
    Be your generous self
and look to what I am.
    Keep your focus on me,
my troubles, help me soon.
    Find me, God, buy me back
from the storehouse of death.
    You know, you see, how they
abuse, shame, disgrace me.
    They have hollowed me out
and made my courage sick;
    and for relief, no one!
for sympathy, no one!
    They fed me poisoned food,
gave vinegar to drink.
    Make food a trap for them.

(over)

And friends a treachery.
  Make them blind in the eye
and shaky in the knee.
  Drown them in your anger,
flash floods of your fury.
  Strip their camps bare as bones,
leave not a soul alive.
  They used your punishment
of me as their excuse
  to add to it their own
and lie about my pain.
  Indict them, crime on crime,
so they never see you,
  erase them from the scroll,
the scroll of lasting life,
  erase them from the just.
May God give me the strength,
  in my grief, in my pain,
to sing a hymn of praise,
  a hymn of thanks to God.
Better this than offer
  a bull, an ox entire.
You others who suffer,
  be happy you seek God,
be courageous again.
  The victim can be heard.
The devotee of God
  is not despicable.
You the earth, you the sky,
  you the sea, you that live
therein, give praise to God.
  For God will save Sion,

God will remake Judah,
  God will call exiles back,
God's children's children will
  have the land as their own,
and they will live in it
  who love the name of God.

Psalm 70

PSALM 70

Help me, God, quickly,
  God, defeat, drive off
those who would kill me,
  who would ruin me,
make them look like fools,
  get rid of them for
their wicked jeering,
  but those who love you,
give them cause for joy,
  and those who love your
saving ways, cause to
  say, "Magnificent!"
But I am helpless!
  Help me, quickly, God,
you are my one way,
  you, my one escape!

PSALM 75

We thank you, God,
   for your just ways.
You are near us.
   We say it, God,
in praise of you.

I will summon the court.
   I will be a just judge.
Even if the earth quakes
   and its people quiver,
I will hold them firm.
   "Do not bellow," I say,
"do not bellow like bulls
   and toss your wicked horns.
Do not toss them at God
   whose power is supreme.
Try nothing against God,
   our everlasting Rock.
God has won the battle,
   east, west, from the desert
south to the mountains north.
   God is the final judge
of who lives and who dies.
   God keeps at hand a bowl
of wine filled to the top,
   and draws wrath from this bowl.
They drink it to the dregs,
   the wicked of the earth,
to the last bitter drop."
   To you, eternal God,
to you, God of Jacob,
   I sing a hymn of praise.

"I will break the forces
of evil and I will
build the forces of good."

Psalm 76

PSALM 76

You proved yourself
    the lion of Judah,
a fearsome name
    to all in Israel.
You made your den
    Jerusalem, Sion.
From there you broke
    attacks, the bow, the shield,
the sword, the rest
    of the weapons of war.
God of great light,
    you are blinding to see.
Attackers tried
    to storm your lion's den,
your mountain lair.
    They stormed to their own deaths,
vanished from sight,
    powerful men, but dead.
They froze in fear
    when you let out a roar,
God of Jacob,
    chariot, horse, they froze!
You are fearsome,
    who could face your fury,
your long standing fury?
    You will roar your
verdict down from the sky,
    the earth will quake,
and they grow still with fright
    when judgment comes
and you stand on behalf
    of the earth's poor,

(over)

and those who survive your
    punitive rage
will be grateful to you
    for righting wrongs.
They will form around you.
    Promise your God
faith and keep your promise.
    Let those with God
offer thanks to the One
    who sees all things,
who knows the wiles of war
    and is fearsome
to peoples who wage it.

PSALM 78

I want you all to hear
    what I have to tell you,
a story from the past
    with a lesson to it,
a past we learned about
    from people before us,
a past we must hand on
    to people after us,
the story of God's deeds,
    marvels and miracles,
glorious works of God!
    We have a law from God,
and each generation
    must teach it to the next,
so that the next in turn
    may teach the not yet born
and they once born may teach
    the children they beget
to put all hope in God
    and never once forget
the things that God has done
    and so to keep the law,
and not be like the past
    peopled with rebellion,
peopled with betrayal
    and souls no God could trust.

The Ephraimites left God
    and ran from the battle,
they were coward bowmen.
    They failed to keep their oath
and do as God had said.

(over)

For they forgot the past,
the things that God had done,
    marvels and miracles
in plain sight of people,
    split the sea, led them through,
the water like a dike.
    God led them with a cloud
by day turned fire by night,
    then split a desert rock
and gave the sand a drink,
    opened crags of water
to run like rivers down.
    But they kept to their sin,
the arid defiance
    of their God overhead.
They made the test of God,
    food to fill their bellies,
with cynical remarks:
    "Can God serve us dinner
out here in the desert?
    God struck open a rock,
it is true, and water
    tumbled down in torrents.
Can God give bread and meat
    to a starving people?"
God's anger at them flared,
    against Jacob, against
Israel, like a fire,
    because they were faithless,
they doubted God's power.
    But God whistled up clouds
and broke them open and

rained manna down on them.
They ate out of the air.
Mortals ate deathless food
full to overflowing.
Then God unleashed the winds,
the east out of its sky,
the south out of its stalls,
and birdflesh fell on them
like dust storms, and piled up
like sand along the sea.
God made the birds fall right
on their camp, on their tents.
So they ate to the full.
They got what they wanted.
But that did not stop them.
They complained with full mouths.
Then God rose in anger
and killed the best of them,
Israel in flower.
God made their lives vanish
quicker than mist, quicker
than a ghost on the run.
Slaughter made them sorry,
made them turn back to God.
They remembered then that
God was their mountain strong,
God was their redeemer.
But they were not sincere.
They flattered God with lies.
They were weak in their will
to believe in God's law.
But God who is mercy

(over)

forgave them for their sin
and did not wipe them out.
  The anger seldom showed,
the rage was seldom fired.
  For they were flesh, God knew,
like a breath, quick and gone.
  Many the time they caused
God grief in the desert
  with their rebellious stands.
They asked for it over
  and over. They prodded
Israel's Holy God.
  They forgot the power,
the time God got them free
  from those who held them down,
the things done in Egypt,
  the things done in Zoan,
marvels and miracles.
  God turned rivers to blood,
they were poison to drink.
  God sent flies to bite them,
the people of Egypt,
  and frogs to smother them,
and grasshoppers to eat
  them bare, and locusts
to strip their harvest fields.
  God killed their vines with hail,
their sycamores with frost,
  killed their cattle with hail,
their sheep with lightning bolts,
  God ablaze with anger,
on a rampage against

them to wreak great havoc.
And to prepare the way,
    pestilential spirits!
God gave them no quarter.
    The plagues were meant to kill.
Egypt's first born children
    were struck down, the fruit of
Egypt's fertility.
    Then God freed our people,
led them out like a flock
    across the trackless waste.
God kept them safe and sound
    while the sea drowned pursuit.
Then to the holy place
    God had chosen for them,
ridding it of others,
    allotting ours the land,
settling in their regions
    each tribe of Israel.
Still they risked God's anger.
    They refused to obey.
The broke with God's commands
    the way their parents did,
snapped like a faulty bow,
    built shrines on high places,
worshiped idols on them,
    infuriating God,
a jealous God who knew
    and got angry enough
to reject Israel,
    to abandon Shiloh,
the tent of the presence

(over)

of God to humankind.
God abandoned the ark,
  gave the glorious ark
into enemy hands.
  It was an angry God
who slaughtered our people
  with an enemy sword.
Young men went up in flames;
  young women stayed unwed;
the priests were hacked to death;
  no widow lived to wail.
God woke as if from sleep,
  as if from being drunk,
woke as a warrior,
  struck the enemy rear
and brought them down in shame.
  God rejected Joseph,
God rejected Ephraim,
  chose the tribe of Judah,
chose beloved Sion.
  God built a holy place
firm as the sky above,
  firm as the earth below,
made to last forever.
  God chose faithful David
from out among the flocks,
  from shepherding sheep to
shepherding God's people,
  Jacob and Israel,
the heritage of God.
  David did, with pure heart.
David did, with pure hands.

PSALM 79

O God, heathen armies took your treasured
    people.
They fouled your temple mount. They tore
    Jerusalem
to pieces stone by stone. They left our dead to
    rot
as carrion for birds, left their innocent flesh
as fodder for wild beasts. They spilled blood
    like water.
There was no one left to bury Jerusalem!
Neighbors treat us like dirt, objects of
    mockery,
objects of ridicule. God! How long will this
    last,
this anger of yours last, this jealousy like fire?
Turn your anger on those who deny what you
    are,
who refuse you as God. They swallowed us
    alive,
shattered us house and home! Do not judge us
    guilty
of the sins of the past. Come quickly, come
    gently,
our lives are at low ebb. God of our lives, help
    us,
free us, so the world knows your name is
    merciful.
Forgive us for mercy or the heathen will say:
"What happened to their God?" Let them
    know what happened,
avenge the blood they shed! We, their
    prisoners, beg

(over)

you to listen, to fight for us or we are dead!
Multiply mockery back on our neighbors'
    heads
for the mockery they made of you, Lord Our
    God!
We will hand on from life to life our thanks to
    you!

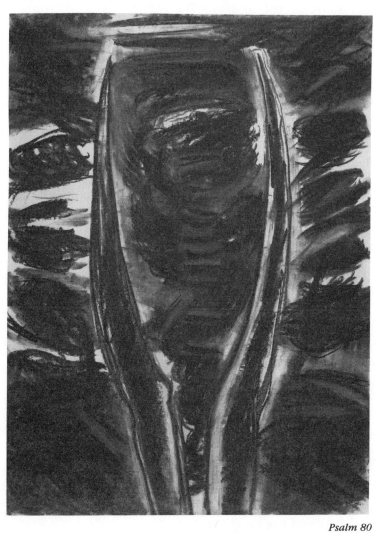

Psalm 80

PSALM 80

We beg you to treat us
   as your flock, O Shepherd
of Israel, to be
   a beacon for Ephraim,
Benjamin, Manasseh,
   to unleash your power
and rush to our rescue!
   Turn back to us, O God,
show us a different face
   so we know we are safe.
Will you nurse your anger
   in spite of our prayers,
God of power and might?
   You made us sup with tears,
swallow tears by the bowl.
   You made us a mockery
to the tribes around us,
   clowns to our enemies.
Turn back to us, O God,
   show us a different face
so we know we are safe.
   We were the vine you brought
out of Egypt. You cleared
   the land of people and
planted us, rooted out
   others and set us down
so we filled the region,
   we cloaked the mountains and
lofty cedars in shade.
   You let our branches reach
to the sea and river.
   Then why cut down our hedge

so all can steal our fruit?
　Wild boars tore us apart,
animals ate us out.
　Turn back to us, O God
of power, we beg you!
　See us from your far away,
come and look at your vine.
　Care for what your power
made, your vine, and the king
　you made strong in your place.
Use your wrath to ruin
　those who made a roaring
bonfire of your people.
　Favor the king, the one
you made strong in your place.
　We never betrayed you.
Put life back in us so
　we may invoke your name.
Turn back to us, O God,
　God of power and might,
show us a different face
　so we know we are safe.

PSALM 81

Shout it, your joy to God!
   Shout it, to Jacob's God,
our fortress, our triumph!
   Sing it, drum the drum, pluck
it strong on harp and lyre.
   Let the brass greet the moon,
full moon, the solemn feast!
   Let Israel obey
the law of Jacob's God!
   God laid it on us all
the time we left Egypt.
   "I heard your voices plead
when you were not yet mine.
   I freed your backs from hods,
freed your hands from hauling.
   You prayed in each crisis.
I saved you, from far off,
   where thunder has its home,
though you made me angry
   near Meribah's waters!
Hear me, O Israel,
   my people, I will give
you the whole truth if you
   will just hear me say it:
Take no alien god
   as your own, no stranger!
I am your God! I brought
   you out of Egypt's land!
I fed your hungry mouths!
   But you went deaf on me
Israel, you dropped me.
   I abhorred your hard hearts.

I let you fool yourselves.
   If you would face the truth,
Israel, and obey,
   I would turn violent
on those who menaced you,
   would finish them off fast!
Whoever opposed me
   would buckle before me,
forever doomed to death.
   But you I would nourish
on the finest wheat and
   on the soul of honey!

PSALM 83

My God, no God can match you!
Do not stay mute and aloof!
Look! An attack is brewing,
the enemy rears his head,
concocts plans to war on us,
the people you so treasure.
"Come, let us wipe them all out!"
they say. "The name Israel,
make it a forgotten word!"
They all have one thing in mind
for the alliance they form,
Edomites, Ishmaelites,
Byblites and Amalekites,
Philistines and Tyrians.
Assyrians have joined them.
Lot's children now have great force!
End them as Midian did,
as Sisera, as Jabin
did at the river Kishon,
gone from the face of the earth,
fertilizer for the fields.
End their chiefs up as Oreb
and Zeeb, chiefs like Zebah
and Zalmunna who said: "Seize
their fattest fields for ourselves!"
End them, God, like tumbleweed,
like chaff scattered to the wind!
Like flames that burn a forest,
like flames that burn a mountain,
storm after them, harass them
like a hurricane, make their
faces pale with craven fear,

and you, God, take your revenge!
Let them lead lives of endless
degradation and torment,
then let them perish in shame.
Make them know that you are God,
you alone, God of the world!

Psalm 84

PSALM 84

What beauty there is
   to your place on earth,
God of power and might!
   My flesh, my spirit
crave to be with you,
   their longings are loud,
living, living God!
   The least sparrow has
a home, the swallow
   a nest for her young
and herself, O God
   of power and might,
God, my Lord and King!
   What a joy they have
who live in your house,
   who sing your praises
day in and day out!
   What a joy for those
who hide in you and
   sing your heartfelt thanks!
     *****

May God the giver
   of rain make brooks flow
along the valley,
   make it all one spring!
May God the thunder
   make it all one pool!
May pilgrims travel
   village to village
to visit the God
   of gods on Sion.
     *****

(over)

Heed me, mighty God
    of Jacob, heed me!
Look at me, I am
    your anointed king!
One day of life lived
    with you is better
than a thousand days
    of life without you.
One day at your door
    is better, O God,
than a thousand days
    in the house of death!
        * * * * *

God is like the sun,
    The Lord, the giver
of life and glory.
    And giver of rain,
the Lord, to people
    who lead holy lives.
What a joy they have
    who put their trust in
you, almighty God!

PSALM 87

The God who loves you,
    the God who built you
on sacred mountains,
    O Gates of Sion,
the God who fashioned
    fair cities for us,
that God speaks in you,
    O City of God:
"I will list monstrous
    Egypt and monstrous
Babylon among
    those who confess me,
even Palestine,
    with Tyre and with Cush:
'They are her children.'"
    But about Sion
it will be said: "All
    life is born from her,
and God the Most High
    will keep her secure."
God will list peoples:
    "They are her children."
And all who suffered
    on our account will
sing and dance in you.

PSALM 89

Do I keep up the song
 about your love, God, keep
saying you are faithful,
 no matter what happens!
I could rattle it off:
 "Everlasting God, your
love is firm as the skies
 you made, your faithfulness
is firmer still than they."
 You said: "I chose the man
and made a pact with him.
 I swore to my David:
'I will make it happen,
 your line of kings will last,
your throne from age to age,'"
 The gods of the sky who
form your court praise the pact,
 praise the firmness of it,
for who can match you there,
 God, which god could come close?
You are fearsome to them,
 even together, you
loom larger than them all.
 God, God of great power,
who is a match for you?
 Heaven forms around you!
You mounted the sea's back.
 You reined in its storm waves.
You made Chaos a corpse.
 One stroke scattered your foes.
Yours the sky, yours the earth,
 yours the world of creatures,

you were their beginning.
　　And the mountains you made,
Zaphan and Amanus,
　　Tabor and Hermon, sing
with joy to be near you.
　　You have warrior strength,
left hand and right hand both,
　　held high in victory!
You are just, you are fair,
　　you are love, you are truth,
these are your throne and court.
　　Those who know your beauty,
God, are favored people,
　　your sunlight to their ways,
happy the day with you,
　　ecstatic with your gifts.
The real glory is yours.
　　We win through your powers.
Our real sovereign is you,
　　Israel's Holy One!
In a vision once you
　　said to a man of faith:
"I made a boy the king,
　　not a warrior man,
the boy, not the hero.
　　I found David and I
marked him with holy oil.
　　I will be his power,
my hand, my arm, his strength.
　　No one will dare face him,
no viciousness beat him.
　　I will smash those who try,

(over)

129

the forces of hatred.
  I will back him fiercely
and through me he shall win,
  to the sea on his left,
the river on his right.
  He will shout it out: 'you
are father to me, God,
  you the strength that saved me!'
I will make him my heir,
  the king of earthly kings.
I will back him for good,
  stick to the oath I swore,
keep his line on the throne,
  his rule like paradise.
If his people refuse
  and violate my law,
refuse and violate
  what I prescribed for them,
I will strike the rebels,
  lash out at their malice,
but never cease backing
  him, never fail my oath.
My covenant will stand,
  my word will not alter.
It is a holy oath
  I swore, good forever,
not a lie to David!
  His lineage will last
until the crack of doom,
  his throne last like the sun,
and like the moon the life
  of his people, and his
rule firmer than the sky!"
  Yet you in your anger,

in your rage at David,
  you broke your word to him,
you profaned his kingship,
  made a breach in his walls,
made his fortress rubble,
  made him pickings for thieves,
a thing his neighbors mocked,
  took away his aura
with the army and threw
  his kingship in the trash.
You made him early old,
  sterile as a young man.
O God, Conquering God,
  how long will you be gone?
How long on fire with rage?
  Think how short, how grievous
my life is! Did you make
  us to end up empty?
Does anyone dodge death,
  get free of the clutch of
Sheol by their own strength?
  God, where is the rescue
you promised earlier
  in your pact with David?
Think of the mockery
  I bear, every pagan
puts a cut in my heart.
  It is you they mock in
me, you when they demean
  the one you chose as yours!

God be praised forever!
  Amen. Amen.

Psalm 92

PSALM 92

The joy it is to sing
you praises, God most high,
   sing you thanks for what you
are, at sunrise to your
   love, at sunset and through
the watches of the night
   to your fidelity,
to the pluck of the lyre,
   the zither and the harp.
For you give me joy, God,
   in all the things you do.
My song is about you,
   your immense creation,
your mind too deep to plumb.
   People can be stupid,
be foolish and forget
   that when sin grew like weeds
and sinners abounded,
   God wiped them out for good.
You are always supreme,
   eternal God, you see
your enemies perish
   and the wicked scattered.
But you let me exult
   as a wild ox, gave me
the sweet smell of success.
   I saw those who slandered
me routed, evil men,
   and I heard the song sung:
Those who keep faith will grow
   like the palm tree, like the

(over)

cedar of Lebanon,
    and when brought to God's house
and planted in God's court,
    they will mature nobly.
Their foliage will be
    fresh and green to old age.
They will show the world how
    just, how sinless God is,
how like a mountain strong.

PSALM 94

God of past revenges,
   God of past revenges,
rise now, judge the judges,
   make them pay for their pride!
The wicked, the wicked,
   how long will you let them
boast of their evil deeds,
   all of them, in public.
They beat your people down,
   God, your precious people,
widow, stranger, orphan,
   murdered them, murdered them,
muttering: God is blind,
   Jacob, God is busy.
Learn, you fools, you dumb fools,
   figure it out yourselves:
Is the God who made ears
   and the God who made eyes
gone deaf and blind to you?
   The master of nations
not able to punish you?
   The teacher of peoples
not able to pick you out?
   God knows your empty heads!
Those you teach your law, God,
   those you form are made full.
They are consoled after
   the bad days are over.
The wicked get a grave!
   We know you will not leave
your people derelict,
   lose your prize possession.

(over)

The bar of justice will
　　right the balance and
restore the heart to hope.
　　Who else took a stand for
me against wickedness
　　and worship of false gods?
If you had not, I would
　　have been in death's dungeon.
Your love kept me alive
　　when I thought I was dead.
At the pitch of my grief
　　your graces calmed my soul.
Can a rogue judge be kin
　　to you, a lawless judge
be under your mantle?
　　They ganged up on the good,
made the guiltless guilty
　　in their secret sessions.
But you stood between us,
　　you, my mountain of strength.
You shot their own malice
　　back at them, God our God.
It devastated them!
　　It devastated them!

PSALM 99

God looms over all
  on clouds of spirits!
People should quiver
  and the earth should quake!
God is far too great
  for Sion, far too
great for earthen gods!
  Let each say of your
great and gracious God:
  "God is holy!"
Monarch of monarchs,
  eager for justice,
you founded fairness,
  you fashioned fairness
for Jacob yourself.
  Praise God to the skies!
Bow down to the earth,
  the footstool of God,
"God is holy!"
  Moses and Aaron
were among your priests,
  Samuel someone
who invoked your name.
  They prayed to you, God,
and you answered from
  the pillar of cloud.
They kept your commands,
  kept the law you gave.
You, God our God, you
  spoke to them, you were
the God who forgave
  them, though you were the

(over)

God who punished them,
   the judge of us all!
Praise God to the skies!
   Bow down to the earth,
the holy mountain
   of our God, for God,
our God, is holy!

PSALM 101

I keep on chanting
  to you, God, chanting
your love, your justice.
  I keep on chanting
your rule over me.
  Will you never come?
I have kept my heart
  clean as ruler here.
I have never prayed
  before a nothing.
I hated idols,
  the making of them
meant nothing to me.
  I was no one's friend
who schemed up evil.
  I stopped malicious
tongues from backbiting.
  I put an end to
proud and haughty ways.
  I chose people of
faith to live with me,
  people of clean life,
they alone were staff.
  No one made empty
idols in my court.
  Liars did not stay
long in my presence.
  I chased from the land
all who love idols,
  chased them like cattle.
I purged them all from
  the city of God.

PSALM 106

Alleluja!
God is our good, give thanks,
　for God is bound to us.
Who has soul enough to
　tell the tale of God's might?
The one who is alive
　to what is right and just.
Make me alive, O God,
　with your gracious power.
Live in me, heal my soul
　so I may share the grace
you give to your people,
　share the joy, the beauty,
you give your descendants.
　We are one with our past.
We sin, we commit crimes.

Once free of Egypt, our
forebears forgot your work,
　your wealth of love for them.
Once across the Reed Sea,
　they got bold with you though
you had gotten them free
　for love's sake, and to show
the power you possessed.
　You dried the Sea, you dried
the Reeds, you led them through
　the trough on desert sand.
You freed them from mortal
　blows, mortal enemies.
The enemy army
　drowned, not a one survived.

They believed what you said
    then, and shouted their thanks.
But they forgot you fast
    and took no more advice.
They put bitter complaints
    to you in the barrens.
You gave them food they asked,
    you filled their scrawny throats.
There were factions in camp
    against Moses, against
Aaron, your holy one.
    The earth opened, swallowed
Dathan whole, then it closed
    and swallowed Abiram.
Faction went up in flames,
    the wicked were burned alive.
They made a calf from brass,
    at Horeb, to adore,
gave up true worship for
    a grass eating, brass bull.
They forgot you, their God,
    things you did in Egypt
for them, things you did in
    Ham, then near the Reed Sea,
all miraculous things.
    You willed to wipe them out.
You would have if Moses,
    your chosen had not stood
in the space between you
    to keep your rage from them.
They refused to believe
    real the land you promised.

(over)

They hunkered in their tents,
  would hear nothing you said.
Your hand rose to scatter
  them, there in the desert,
far and wide through foreign
  peoples and places.
They hooked themselves up with
  the Baal of Peor and
ate the food of the dead.
  This got you so angry
you sent a plague on them.
  But Phinehas pleaded
and the plague disappeared
  because he was holy,
so people have thought from
  his generation down.
At Meribah, at the
  waters, they provoked you.
That cost Moses. He said
  faithless things when they did
not accept his vision.
  They did not kill the conquered
as you had ordered them.
  They mixed in marriage and
took on enemy ways,
  made up to their idols,
so seductive they were,
  butchered for the demon's
sake their sons and daughters.
  It was innocent blood
they shed, their own childrens',
  to placate the idols

of Canaan. They fouled the
   land with rivers of red.
They were filthy for it,
   they whored for those idols.
Again your anger blazed,
   you loathed your heritage.
So you put your people
   into pagan bondage,
under enemy rule.
   They were treated badly,
stripped of their dignity.
   You freed them and freed them
but they fixed on evil
   and fell from their own crimes.
You kept faith with them.
   Your rich love drew them on.
Before their captors' eyes
   your love worked to free them.

God, our God, preserve us,
   pluck us from the pagans,
we want to reverence
   your name wherever we
are, whenever we pray.
   Thank God, Israel's God,
forever, forever!
   Say "amen!" to this, "amen!"
Alleluja!

PSALM 108

My love is strong, God.
  I will chant it.
Come alive my heart,
  alive my harp,
to make the dawn live.
  I will sing thanks
to you, God, though I
  be with pagans
in pagan places.
  Your love is large
as heaven, your faith
  large as the sky.
You are beyond our
  reach, your beauty
broods over the earth.
  Use your power.
Make me win the war
  so the king you
love may be preserved.

  The oracle
God spoke to him is:
  "I will be glad
to make Shechem mine,
  to leave my mark
on Succoth Valley.
  Mine Gilead
and mine Manasseh.
  Ephraim my
helmet, Judah my
  battle baton,

Moab my wash bowl.
 I will trample
Edom underfoot.
 I will roar and
take Philistia."

 Who will capture
Petra for me, make
 me Edom's king?
And you, God, do you
 stay angry with
us and not campaign
 ever again
with our men at war?
 You be our help
against enemies.
 Human help is
futile against them.
 With you we win.
You will trample down
 those who face us.

PSALM 109

Do not go deaf to me,
   God, not to this:
People mouth and mouth
   malicious lies
against me, their maws wide,
   tongues out, words, lies,
they snap all around me.
   They have no cause.
I treated them as friends.
   They pay me back
in slander, yes me, me!
   They think me bad
to pray—good gains evil,
   love gains hatred.

Let Satan prosecute
   him to his face,
the verdict be guilty,
   his plea a sin!
Let him die soon, lose his
   job to someone!
Orphan his children and
   widow his wife!
Beggar his brood for good,
   have their homes seized!
Take his estate for debt,
   gobble it up!
Show him no pity, none
   to his orphans!
Blot his future out, blot
   his life to come!

May God never forget
    his father's sins!
May God never forgive
    his mother's sins!
May God use them as cause
    to blot this man
from mortal memory,
    pitiless man,
a hound to the helpless,
    a killer of
people already killed.
    He loved curses.
They come back to haunt him.
    He loathed blessings.
They are gone out of reach.
    Curses were like
clothes he wore, like water
    for his belly,
like a balm for his bones.
    So swathe him in
them, day in and
day out, as with a belt!
    And the others,
the evil-mouthed, lying mouthed
    others, God pay
them in a thousand shames
    for harming me!
Then help me, God, my God,
    some miracle,
for the goodness you are,
    out of pity,

(over)

get me free, I am down
    and out, I am
cut to the heart by this.
    I am shadow
thin, and as quickly gone.
    My youth is up,
my old age is with me.
    I am shaky
from fasting, my flesh gone
    from full to spare.
I am a mockery
    to those I meet.
Their heads shake in disgust.
    Help me, my God,
free me for pity's sake,
    so people know
yours is the hand at work,
    you have done it!
Let them curse me, if you
    bless me; let them
rise, if you make them fall
    and me rejoice.
Clothe liars in disgrace,
    dress them in shame.
From my mouth will come thanks
    to the Great God.
From my age will come praise,
    for God will back
the victim, and save him
    from a bad judge.

PSALM 110

God, to my King, an Oracle:
   "Sit at my right.
I will make your throne,
   your footstool,
the backs of your enemies."

God forged you a winning weapon,
   the God of Sion,
   hammer and tongs,
God your strength battling
   your enemies,
your courage the day you conquered.
When the Holy One showed,
   it was courage for you,
   like dawn, like dew,
   it was life for you.

God swore to you,
   and will not revoke it:
     "You are a priest
     of the eternal God,
   as God has sworn it.
     You are a king,
     God's rightful king, my Lord,
   as you have sworn it."
The God who routed armies
   when enraged,
left stacks of corpses,
struck heads off left and right.
This God seats a king.
This God lifts a King's head high.

Psalm 118

PSALM 118

Give the good God thanks,
  "God backs us forever!"
Say it Israel,
  "God backs us forever!"
Say it Aaron,
  "God backs us forever!"
All you that heed God,
  "God backs us forever!"

From the pit of Death, I called God.
From the pitch of Life, God replied.
God is for me. I am fearless.
Who can harm me? God is for me.
My great fighter. I can see them
all collapse, all my enemies.
Better the backing of God than
the backing of mortal princes.
Hostile forces all around me!
With God my cry, I slaughtered them.
On every side, on every side!
With God my cry, I slaughtered them.
Swarming like bees, crackling like fire
at burning thorns, on every side!
With God my cry I slaughtered them.
You, grim death, had me to the brink.
But God braced me. God was my fort,
God was my guard, my victory.
Mine was the camp that exulted.
God's was the might that prevailed.
The mighty arm, the mighty arm
of God was lifted in triumph!
I was not killed, I lived to tell

(over)

the day, to tell the deeds of God.
God let me suffer severely
for it, but did not let me die.

Open victory
   the gates, let me enter
them to give God thanks.
   This is the gate of God
for victors only.
   My thanks. You won for me,
you were the triumph.
   You made the cornerstone
what the masons ditched.
   God has made this happen,
a marvel to see.
   This day the deeds are God's.
Be glad, glad in God!

   Give us victory, God,
we beg you. Send us
   good days, God we beg you.
May God keep the one
   who comes in God's name, we
pray it in God's house.
   Let green branches adorn
the sanctuary,
   the horns of the altar.
You are God, my God,
   I thank you, I praise you.

Give the good God thanks,
   "God backs us forever!"

PSALM 119

ALEPH

How wonderful the life
  led by the law you gave.
And they are wonderful
  who live that ordered life,
who search out what you want,
  who never commit sin,
but keep to the right road.
  You asked us to observe
with care what you command.
  I wish I led a life
that could match what you ask.
  I could study your ways
without feeling ashamed.
  As I learn to be just,
I praise how just you are.
  I will do what you say.
Do not leave me alone,
  God, you are lasting life.

BETH

How can the young stay pure?
  By the path of your law.
My heart is after you.
  Do not let it wander.
I keep myself from sin
  by loving your vision.
Accept my deep thanks, God,
  teach me your traditions.

(over)

I will tell the whole world
　　every word you utter.
My joy is not in wealth
　　but in your ordered way.
Keep it before my mind.
　　Keep it before my eyes.
My joy is in your law,
　　to remember your words.

GIMEL

Give me the means to live
　　so I may obey you.
Give me the eyes to see
　　the beauty of order.
My life on earth is brief,
　　reveal your law to me.
I want your commandments.
　　I want them all the time.
Punish those damnable
　　people who scoff at law,
rid me of their catcalls
　　for keeping your commands.
Let them gripe about me.
　　I keep my mind on you.
Your laws are my delight,
　　like counsellors to me.

DALETH

I am face down in death.
　　Make me live! You promised!
You fulfilled what I preached.
　　Teach me more about you,

the way you order things,
    so I can wonder more.
A sorrow weighs me down.
    Stand me straight! You promised!
Steer me far from falsehood,
    grace my life with your law.
I want the life of truth.
    I prize your way as best.
I have held firm to it,
    God, keep me from failing.
The more I understand,
    the more I will obey.

HE

Teach me obedience
    to your rule of life, God,
the rich reward of it.
    Let me know it enough
to give it my whole heart,
    the straight and narrow path
that gives me great delight.
    March me to your commands
away from lawless gain.
    Distract me from idols
with your living power.
    Hold good to your promise
for I have obeyed you.
    People blame me for it.
I respect you because
    your rule of life is good.
Look at my love for it.
    Answer love with life.

(over)

WAW

Let me sense your love, God,
　　you said it would save me.
My response to abuse
　　will be trust in your word.
Do not permit the truth
　　to leave my speech, O God!
I hang on what you say
　　so I can obey you
as long as you are God,
　　so I can live at large
while I search for your will,
　　so I can tell your law
to the powers that be
　　and not look like a fool.
I will relish the words
　　of your law which I love
and lift my hands to you
　　as your beloved laws say.
They are my food for thought.

ZAIN

Please keep your word to me.
　　I base my hope on it,
that it keep me alive,
　　comfort me in crisis.
The lawless mock at me,
　　God forever and ever!

I never leave your law.
   It is my solace, God,
to know your ancient rule.
   I am enraged by those
who leave your law to sin.
   Your commands keep me safe
as I pass through this life.
   I think of you all night,
God, think of your commands.
   I was treated with scorn
because I obeyed them.

HETH

I will obey your laws,
   God my maker, I swear.
I truly need your grace,
   keep your word to save me.
I saw what you required
   so I remade my life.
I remade it quickly
   to conform to your law.
And I kept obeying
   though sinners crowded me.
At midnight I get up
   to thank you for just ways.
I am a kindred soul
   to those who respect you,
to those who keep your law.
   You fill the earth with love,
God, teach me loving ways.

(over)

TETH

God, give me the goodness
    that is found in your words.
Teach me to know and judge.
    I believe in your way.
I was lawless before
    but law abiding now.
You are the good you cause.
    Teach me your traditions.
Scofflaws smear me with lies,
    still, still I obey you.
Ignorance dullens them,
    still, still, I love your way.
Some good came from my pain.
    I learned your commandments.
The instructions you give
    mean more to me than coin,
stacks of silver and gold.

YODH

You shaped me with your hands.
    Give me also the light
to know what you command.
    Those who live by your word
will rejoice to see me
    leading my life by you.
I know you do just things,
    God, and you caused me pain
to bring me to the truth.
    Let what is kind in you

comfort me, as you said,
   and let your compassion
come and keep me alive.
   I love your law of life.
Disgrace those who hate it!
   They tried to make me sin,
but I kept you in mind.
   Let those who live by you
look to me for your law.
   May my conscience stay pure
and myself free of shame.

KAPH

I wait so long, so long
   for help, for word to come,
my eyes blur with watching.
   "When will I know comfort?"
I weep as if from smoke,
   yet keep your love in mind.
"How long will my life be?
   When will you punish those
who are harrassing me?"
   They want to make me sin
who sin against your law.
   They ruin me with lies.
Your commands are truth.
   Help me! I was almost
gone but I still obeyed
   the law of life you gave.
Keep me in your kindness
   so I may keep your law.

(over)

LAMEDH

Your word is lasting, God,
    more than the sky above.
You fixed the truth for us
    from life to life to life.
It will outlast the earth.
    All things are your creatures
You decide if they live.
    Pain would have ruined me
without your law to love.
    I will not let it go.
Your law keeps me alive.
    Save what is yours to save
for I am your servant.
    Malicious people plot
my death for being so,
    but I keep to your law.
Your way is more perfect
    than any way I know,
O God, our final end.

MEM

I love your way, love it,
    think on it all the time.
It gives me a wisdom
    my enemies have not
because it stays with me.
    I surpass my teachers.
I meditate on you.
    I surpass my elders.

I obey your commands.
  I avoid evil ways
so I can keep to yours.
  I stay with what you ask
for you taught me yourself.
  Your words are sweet to taste,
they are sweet in my mouth.
  I know the truth through you,
God of absolute truth.
  I hate ways that are false.

NUN

Your words are like a lamp
  I see by in the dark.
I will hold to my word
  to obey your just laws.
I am dead empty God,
  keep your word to save me.
Grace me with your great thoughts,
  instruct me in your way.
I live in your lasting hands.
  I am mindful of you.
Wicked people try to
  trick me into sinning
but I do not succumb.
  Your law is an heirloom
that fills my heart with joy,
  O everlasting God!
I am eager to live
  the kind of life you want.
It gains a lasting prize.

(over)

SAMEKH

I hate duplicity.
   I love what you propose.
You guard me, you guide me.
   I wait on what you say.
And you, the wicked, leave
   me alone to obey
what God demands of me.
   Let me live with your word
to sustain me and not
   be a fool to have hoped.
Guarantee my safety,
   God who lasts forever,
my living of your law.
   Make rubbish of people
who live by other rules
   for they adore false gods.
I love your rule of life.
   You get rid of the dross,
people who commit sin.
   I feel you as a shock.
I fear what you may judge.

AIN

I have a just complaint.
   Plead it for me! Do not
leave me in hostile hands.
   God of goodness, stand strong
for me so the wicked
   will not bring me to grief.

I may go blind before
    I see you come to help
with your promised justice.
    Be your kind self with me,
explain your way of life.
    I am yours, help me see
so I understand you.
    You must do something, God,
they have sinned against you.
    God of absolute truth,
I love your rule of law
    more than I love pure gold.
God of absolute truth,
    I know your way is right.
I hate the way of lies.

PE

Your laws are filled with charm,
    God of absolute truth.
I keep them with my soul.
    Let them blossom like light
to teach the ignorant.
    Wanting your way of life
is like gasping for air.
    Become aware of me.
Show me the compassion
    those who love you have known.
Walk me straight with your word.
    Let no sin strap me down.
Free me from oppression
    so I may live your way.

(over)

Show me your loving face,
   fashion me in your law.
I weep at what I see,
   God, your law is not kept.

SADE

You are a just judge, God,
   you hand down just verdicts.
You were right to impose
   your way of life on us,
impose fidelity
   on us, almighty God.
Those dead set against me
   wanted to wipe me out.
They were blind to your law.
   Your word is a proven
word, God, a word I love.
   Young as I am, hated,
I stay mindful of you.
   You are justice itself,
O God everlasting.
   The truth is in your law.
I took delight in it
   even in grief and pain.
O God everlasting,
   give me to understand
the justice of your way
   so I may keep alive.

QUOPH

With my whole self I prayed:
   God give me what I ask

so I may live your law.
    I begged you to save me
so I could keep your rules.
    I faced the dusk and prayed
and waited for your word.
    I kept my eyes on you
every hour of the night,
    your promises in mind.
Hear my prayer, gracious God.
    Just God, keep me alive.
Idolaters close in,
    foreign to your ways.
But you are closer, God,
    each law of yours is truth.
O God everlasting,
    I submit to your rule
made before time began.

RESH

Feel my pain and free me
    for I kept faith with you.
Take my side, ransom me,
    you gave your word you would.
Keep life from the sinful,
    they do not live your law.
You have forgiven much,
    God, so spare me my life.
It is what you promised.
    Many people hate me,
many persecute me,
    still I keep to your way.
It sickens me to see
    faithless people because

(over)   165

they have no use for you.
   I love your way of life.
Keep me alive in it.
   Your word is truth itself,
O God everlasting,
   your judgment pure justice.

SHIN

They are bad men who hound
   me and have no reason.
I hate their harassment.
   It is a joy to hear
your word, my great solace.
   I loathe, loathe what is false.
I love your way of life.
   I praise how just you are
seven times every day.
   Enrich the lives of those
who love your way of life.
   Let them miss not a step.
I hope for life from you,
   God, so I obey you.
I obey your commands
   out of deep love for them.
I keep your law because
   you see my every act.

TAU

Let my plea reach you, God.
   Give me understanding.

It was what you promised.
　　Give my prayer a hearing.
Save me! You said you would!
　　For the law you taught me,
let me sing your praises.
　　For the justice in it,
let me say it by rote.
　　I chose your way of life.
Please offer me your help.
　　I want my life from you,
God, my joy is in you.
　　I want my soul to live
long so I can praise you.
　　May your law help me live.
If I ever become
　　a lost sheep, look for me.
I will know your summons.

PSALM 120

In time of siege,
    I prayed to God
and God freed me.

    Free me now, God,
from lips that lie,
    from tongues that cheat.

God will pierce you,
    God will burn you,
you cheating tongue!
    like sharp arrows
from an archer,
    like red hot coals
from a broom plant.

    I am bad off!
If I lived near
    distant Mesech
or the distant
    tents of Kedar,
I would still live
    too close to those
here who hate peace!

    I wanted peace.
I said I did.
    They wanted war,
and war alone.

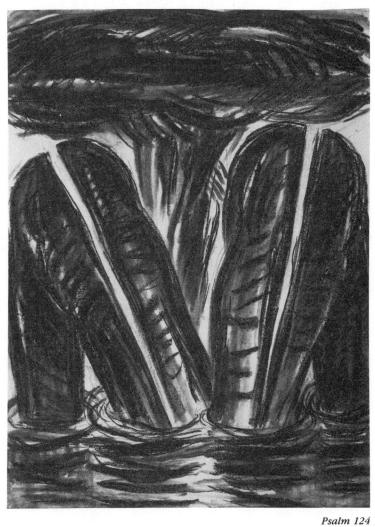

Psalm 124

PSALM 124

God was for us, God was for us,
    say it firmly, Israel!
If not, if not, we were dead, we
    were swallowed live when they rose
against us, men of blazing wrath.
    We were dead in a flash flood
that swept us away, the waters
    of death raging over us.
Thank God who did not make us meat
    for their mouths. We slipped the noose
like a bird from a fowler's trap.
    The trap broke and we are free.
Our safety is in the power
    of God who made earth and sky.

PSALM 125

They will be solid
    as Sion who trust in God.
    The God of Jerusalem
    will never fall.

The hills are all around her,
    as God is all around her,
    for now, for ever.

No evil will rule a land
    of just people unless they
    turn evil themselves.

God, be the goodness of the
    good, the rightness of their hearts.

But for those who play
    both sides, evil and good, may
    God make them vanish with those
    who do straight evil.

PSALM 127

Fools build a temple
   God does not build
Fools guard a city
   God does not guard.
Fools who work early,
   Fools who work late
For sterile profit.
   God will profit
The people God loves.

   The child is God's
Bequest, new born life
   Is God's reward.
Sons you fathered young
   Are like arrows
In a bowman's hand.
   The man who has
His quiver of sons
   Is a safe man.
No one captures him.
   Instead, he drives
Away all attack
   On his city.

Psalm 129

PSALM 129

"I have been downed often
   since I was young!"
Say it Israel:
   "I have been downed often
since I was young,
   but not defeated!
Like plowmen, they put a
   plow to my back
and made the scars long!"

   May the just God smash all
wicked forces
   and drive in retreat
all those who hate Sion.
   Let them be like the hay
a mud roof grows,
   it withers on sight,
not a handful to reap,
   not an armful
to bind into sheaves,
   not a soul to pass and
say: "God's harvest
   be yours! In the name
of the Lord we bless you."

PSALM 132

"God won your battles, David,
    do not forget it!
You swore to God, took an oath
    to Jacob's great God:
'I will not rest in a house,
    not climb to my bed,
I will not let my eyes close,
    not rest them in sleep
before I find a place fit
    for Jacob's great God!' "

"This we heard in Ephrathah,
    in the fields of Jaar.
Up we go to worship God
    where God touches ground."

"Mount to your place of repose,
    God, with your strong ark.
May your priests be holy, your
    people ecstatic.
Do not forget your David,
    hear the king's prayer!"

"God swore to you, David, and
    will not break that oath:
'I will seat someone drawn from
    your flesh on your throne.
If your flesh keeps faith with me,
    follows my commands,
their flesh too will occupy
    your throne forever.

(over)

I have made Sion the place
    where I want to rest,
my place to be forever,
    I want to rule here.
I will reward her pilgrims,
    give food to her poor,
wrap her priests in holiness,
    and people in joy.
I will light and trim David
    as a lamp for her.
Sion's foes will be in rags.
    David's crown will glow.' "

PSALM 135

Alleluja!
For what God is, for what God does!
You in the temple court,
in the Name of our God,
sing it, for God is good,
Alleluja!
Sing God's beautiful Name!
God chose our parent stock
to give it special care
(Israel and Jacob).
Yes, God is great, greater
than all other gods, yes!
God wills it, God does it,
in the air, on the ground
and seas, bottomless seas,
calls up clouds from nowhere,
flicks lightning and makes rain,
leads the winds from their stalls.
God struck Egypt's firstborn
down, man, woman, and beast,
sent warnings to Egypt
against Pharaoh and all
his slavish followers!
God struck mighty nations
down, and killed mighty kings,
Sihon, the Amorite,
and Og of Bashan, yes,
every king of Canaan,
and gave their conquered land
for Israel to keep.
God, for ages to come!
God, for peoples to come!

(over)

A God to defend us,
to show us compassion!
Goldsmith, silversmith, they
make the pagan gods:
who have tongues but are mute,
and have eyes but are blind,
and have ears but are deaf,
and have mouths but not breath.
Like gods, like makers, like
all who believe in them.
Alleluja Israel!
Alleluja Aaron!
Alleluja Levi!
Alleluja everyone
who has respect for God!
To the God of Sion,
Jerusalem's soul,
Alleluja!

PSALM 136

God is our good, give thanks,
 for God is bound to us;
The God of gods, give thanks,
 for God is bound to us;
The Lord of lords, give thanks,
 for God is bound to us;
The single source of life,
 for God is bound to us;
The mind that made the sky,
 for God is bound to us;
Set land upon the sea,
 for God is bound to us;
And great lights overhead,
 for God is bound to us;
The sun, the prince of day,
 for God is bound to us;
Moon, stars, princes of night,
 for God is bound to us;
Killed Egypt's first-born child,
 for God is bound to us;
Led Israel's escape,
 for God is bound to us;
By the sweep of an arm,
 for God is bound to us;
Split the Reed Sea in two,
 for God is bound to us;
Marched Israel across,
 for God is bound to us;
Closed it on Pharaoh's might,
 for God is bound to us;
Brought us through the desert,
 for God is bound to us;

(over)

Smashed peoples in our path,
    for God is bound to us;
Slaughtered their famous kings,
    for God is bound to us;
Sihon, the Amorite,
    for God is bound to us:
Even Og of Bashan,
    for God is bound to us;
Gave us their land to keep,
    for God is bound to us;
For servant Israel,
    for God is bound to us;
God knew we were enslaved,
    for God is bound to us;
Freed us from oppression,
    for God is bound to us;
The God who feeds all flesh,
    for God is bound to us;
To God above, give thanks,
    for God is bound to us.

PSALM 137

The bitter songs we sang as captives
crouched by the river in Babylon,
remember! How we hid our harps in
the thick trees not to play our lyrics
of joy for them. They goaded us, "Sing
something happy, songs about your God!"
It was torment! What lyrics of God
would they not profane if we sang them!
Jerusalem, if I ever do,
may the hand that plays be paralyzed,
and may I choke if I ever, if
you, Jerusalem, do not look proud
worn on my head like a holy wreath
on a holy day! God! Our blood kin
too wanted Jerusalem ruined:
"Strip her down to her last rag of stone!"
Remember! It would be a fierce joy
for me, Babylon, you greedy beast,
to see you sacked ounce for ounce as you
once sacked us, a fierce joy for me if
someone took your young as you did ours
and brained them on rocks!

Psalm 138

PSALM 138

My thanks to you
go deep. I say them though
there are gods here,
my body bowed toward where
your temple is.
My thanks are to your name.
You made it stand
clearly before the world
by your grace, by
your fidelity to
what you promised.
You gave me the battle
when I asked you,
kept me at fever pitch
on the attack.
Now when you speak, every
king everywhere
will submit to you, God.
They will admit
you have power over
them and will say:
"All might belongs to God!"
Who sees how small
I am, yet is the large;
Who hears how close
I am, yet is the far.
Keep me alive
when I face my foes in
savage combat.
Lay your hand left
and right and make me win!
Be my vengeance,

(over)

God, while life is in me.
Your love never
fails, God. Let it never
fail your creature.

Psalm 139

PSALM 139

You be judge, God, you be jury for me!
If I sit, if I stand, you know it first.
If I think thoughts, you know it miles away.
When I travel, you see my starts, my stops,
my steps between. Not a word on my
    tongue—
you know it first. You are close behind me,
close ahead, you can press me with both
    hands.
What you know blinds me, overhead, circling,
I cannot look. Where could I run from you?
Where hide from you? Up the rungs of
    heaven?
I come to you! Down with the dead in hell?
I come to you! If I fly from east to
west, to the lip of the sea, I will fly
in your left hand and settle in your right.
Even at night I know you follow me,
even at night; I am a flood of light
to you; the dark is not dark; it is day;
noon and night shine; you see me by them
    both.
You made me, lung, loin and heart. You kept
    me
alive before I was born then after.
It is you I have to thank, God above,
for filling me with joy at what you make.
I kneel to you! You saw my soul begin,
you see it now, marrow and bone laid bare
by your knowledge. When I was shaped like
    clay
somewhere secret, kneaded like dough deep
    in

the woman-earth, you foresaw it, and each
step since then, all of them logged in your
  book
ahead of time, each day laid out for me
before it came. Your plans are fathomless
to me, O God! infinite in number,
like sand to count grain by grain if I could.
I hope my eyes open forever so
I can see you! God, I hope you wipe out
all wickedness! Let those who trust clay gods
stay clear of me! They talk to foolish lumps,
rows of nothings! Do you not see I loathe
those who loathe you? That I am shocked by
  those
who defy you? I cut them off, they are
poison to me! Be judge, be jury, God!
Weigh my conscience! See how no false god
has ever fooled me! Then you, you take me to
where I will last, where you rule forever!

PSALM 140

Free me from the brutes, God, the vicious
    brutes
whose heart's blood is crime, who think crime
    non-stop.
Razor-tongued, like snakes! Poison-lipped, like
    snakes!
Keep their wicked hands off me, God, ward off
their violence, they want to ruin me!
Thugs that they are, they set their lawless trap
beside my life and bait it against me!
I want you to know: "You are my one God!"
Will you listen, Lord, to this plea for help!
O God, my one God, fortress of my life,
when my battle comes, shield my life for me!
Do not let them do what they want, O God,
mighty God, do not let them spring their trap!
These plagues of my life, drown them in
    venom
drawn from their own mouths! Throw them in
    the fire,
heap hot coals on them forever in hell!
Never let them up from the swamp of death!
Let scandal-mongers lose their right to live!
Let criminals die hounded by their crimes!
I know you protect helpless people, God,
people stripped of their rights. They are the
    ones who
will thank you by name and live in your sight!

Psalm 141

189

PSALM 141

I call and call you, God, come near me now!
Hear my words to you! Take this plea I make
as incense I burn; take these raised hands as
nightly sacrifice. Help me guard my tongue.
Help me watch my words. Let a false promise
never seduce me; let me never join
in the wicked rites people do for their
false gods, never touch a bite of their feasts.
You could punish me, you could rebuke me,
you, God, just and kind, you could keep the
   oils
from blessing my head, but I would still pray
you to halt their crimes. Let their lords fall
   once
into your hands and hear you, they will know
what cold comfort is! You strike and shatter
bones like rocks below. "You fling us broken
at the brink of hell!" But God, my one Lord,
I need your help now. I trust in you. Do
not leave me helpless. Keep me wide of the
trap idolaters rig for me, the lures
they use to catch me! Let their evil trap
spring on them instead. Walk me by them
   free!

Psalm 144

PSALM 144

God be thanked, who fortified me
for combat, trained my hands, my arms
to warfare, God my battlement,
barricade, unbreachable place,
the God I am bound to and trust,
who put the conquered at my feet.

Why care about us?
Why think about us,
God, creatures, creatures?
We are fog and gone,
shadows quick and gone!

God, bend your sky low.
Make the mountains smoke.
Scatter flashes of
lightning, make lightning
arrows, scatter them.
With your two hands pluck
me out of death's lake,
free of ruthless men.
They lie in their teeth.
They swear oaths and lie.

God, let me chant you
a new song on a harp
strung taut with ten strings.
Death has a dagger.
Save me from it, save
me from ruthless men
who lie in their teeth,
who swear oaths and lie.

God shape us men straight as trees from
seedlings, and women like columns
carved to hold palaces in place.
God fill our granaries chock full,
make our sheep teem with lambs choking
our granges, our cattle fatten;
and no siege, no exile, no screams
in our squares.

What a grace to live
such a life! What a grace to have
such a God!

PSALM 149

Cry God!

Cry God anew! Boast God
as you muster belief.
You tribe of God, exult,
you race of God, exult
in your Maker, your King!
Honor your King, and dance
and drum and strike the strings!
We are God's joy, so God
will have us win the war
though we are weak! Cheer this
glorious God, faithful
people! Even asleep,
sing songs of war, glory
words to God in your throats.
But let the sword that cuts
both ways twirl in your hands,
to harrow the heathen,
to pay them back in kind,
shackle their kings, shackle
their chiefs in chains.
They are under sentence
from God. Your honor will
be to carry it out!

Cry God!

I call these psalms tragic because most of them reveal how good people are tempted by goodness itself to become destructive. And that causes them to lose their goodness. Maybe even permanently. Goodness means creativity to me, badness destructivity, and I find these definitions in the psalms themselves. Which only serves to increase their shock effect on me. The psalmists become blind to their own truths.

Surely enough, the psalmists think creativity is the result of order and chaos in conflict, with order winning out. In destructivity chaos wins out. That is what death is, the nearly formless kingdom where everything goes awry. The victory of order is like the victory of a thunderstorm over a drought or of a warrior over an enemy. It may even be for the psalmists that order and chaos switch roles, order being a structure of sinfulness, chaos being a passion for purification. But very quickly the chaos is seen as the return of some original value to a condition that has reversed that value, i.e., the covenant returns to an idolatrous situation. So however destructive the passion of ordering may seem, it is really an attempt to reabsorb what was lost to it. Not to destroy what was lost. This interpretation may seem to read later Bible back into earlier Bible. I do not think so. Every time a psalmist felt permanently lost, felt near to death and chaos, that psalmist saw destructivity as the ultimate evil, even if sin had made death seem like a just punishment. The psalmist appealed against justice itself for the pure gift of life and appealed to a god who lived beyond justice in the realm of mercy. The tragedy is that the psalmists could forget for others what they remembered for themselves, that the ultimate creativity was mercy. Mercy, the power to absorb what is not itself into a life that ultimately cannot be destroyed. It is not like letting the killer inside the door.

How is it possible to forget such a powerful insight and think that goodness must destroy evil, not absorb it, in order to survive? People say enormous suffering will certainly make one forget. Yet there are contrary examples in history, not many, but there, in which a victim absorbs the suffering and the cause of it so that some life survives and the truth appears that vengeance destroys the avenger. It does not purify. People say enormous self-righteousness will make one forget. Also enormous submission in which someone accepts to destroy others by accepting to execute a moral decision made by authorities the someone respects. Also enormous erotic satisfaction which converts the experience of destruction into an experience of creation. Also the yielding to any passion which becomes so intense it seems to purify itself by its very intensity and no longer to know what it is doing outside itself. Also, to name only one more, the identification of the passions of the self with the passions of God because they are for the right things.

Mercy is a passion too. It is even a carnal passion. We need only watch people plead. So I do not identify passion as the culprit which causes good people to become destructive. It is a passion for the self that can make the mistake. Not a passion for the other. When the psalmists are impassioned for their own selves, they envision a God that must be impassioned the same way for God's own self. When the psalmists are impassioned for others, they envision a God who is the same way. It must be said, however, that the psalmists are sometimes impassioned for God against those who blaspheme God, by idolatry, by violation of the covenant, etc. Yet that is not the same as pleading for mercy for someone lost in sin and headed for perdition. They have something of their own at stake in God.

It is one thing for the psalmists to know they cannot absorb the evil inflicted on them, to know they must resort to violence to save themselves or the people to which they belong. It is another thing for them to think their God is like them, to think it without a doubt. The psalmists can also feel what mercy is, as I have mentioned, and can feel that divine mercy is like their own, and feel it without a doubt. So the problem of the psalmists is not that they project human traits onto God. The problem is which ones. Often within a psalm there is a plea for both mercy and revenge run together as though the plea is of a single cloth. I suggest again that their own experience of creation and of mercy could have revealed to them the nature of destructivity and pitilessness. The psalmists have included God in their way of understanding. So there is more to their lives than self-survival at any cost. They sometimes interpreted their own suffering as coming from God, and rightly so they said, for their own sins or the sins of the people. That is when their pleas become most acute.

And yet has God not given the psalmists mixed signals? They describe the *Exodus* as occurring only when God turned violent and forced Egypt to surrender its slaves. They describe their purification in the desert as possible only because of God's punitive wrath. They describe the takeover of the Promised Land as due to violence inflicted by God on the resisting tribes., They describe victory over idolatry as due singly to the wrath of God. Whatever it may mean—their attribution of salvation to God— surely what happened gave them some cause for their conclusions. It is as if they found out from God what "necessary evil" was. The words "necessary evil" evoke a phrase from *Macbeth* who said of his intention to murder Duncan, "we do but teach bloody instructions which being taught return to plague the inventor." The psalmists' generations suffered terribly from the consequences of the "necessary evils" they inflicted. There are several moments when they become aware of this, become aware of their abandonment by God despite all promises to preserve them, through force if necessary. And these several moments are not ones in which they feel justly punished. The opposite in fact. It can seem that God led the psalmists into the trap I have called tragic, giving them to understand that the revenge they wanted was the revenge God wanted, the destruction they begged for was what God wanted to inflict. I am reminded in some way of the plight of Oedipus the King. Here was a man who read his own situations, who made his own choices. Every reading, every choice he made led him to do exactly what was foreordained for him by the god Apollo. And the audience watches this rigged freedom and senses that life could be rigged for it the same way by divine will. Somewhere in all this there lurks what Paul Ricoeur calls the "unavowable theology," that the divine causes human evil. The psalmists, in their own way and with their own imagery, have had to handle that experience. It brought them right up against the question which can be put in Archibald MacLeish's cynical lines from *J.B.*, "If God is god, he is not good. If God is good, he is not God." The psalmists' instincts are to deny that evil comes from God. Yet when the innocent suffer, the pressure to blame God at least for being absent becomes very great. There are times when the psalmists get close to a greater blame. It would be neat enough to recall Plato saying goodness cannot cause evil and to lay the blame for the confusion on the nature of imagery used by dramatists and psalmists alike. Imagery has its reasons for existing. Imagery is not failed thought.

I do not call these psalms tragic simply because I see Greek definitions of tragedy exemplified in them though the psalms are not plays. They are tragic because they miss their own truths. Death is not the cause of life, nor life the cause of death. The one is the victory over the other. Life is not to be abandoned to death. Sin is not to be abandoned to death. And yet the sinner is, the idolater, the pagan, the nations. This latter attitude splits the psalms the way an earthquake splits the ground. We do not have to wait in the tradition of belief until the books of Job and Jonah appear to find a consciousness of that split, nor do we have to wait for the Suffering Servant imagery of Isaiah. My guess is that the psalmists often borrowed from the nations the imagery they used to express an experience of God. So they must have recognized values outside their own. They had a universality handed to them which they knew how to assimilate even if for reasons of spiritual conquest. My guess is also that the psalmists recognized that the stipulations of the covenant referred to all peoples. Just as their sense of God was that their God was the one for all, the Lord of the lesser gods, even if for reasons of spiritual conquest. And there is the imagery of the final times when the renewed Jerusalem is to draw to itself by its God-given beauty all the kings and peoples of the earth. Even the imagery of the Davidic King is the imagery of God the King of all, though it can quickly cease to be a revealing metaphor and become an excuse for narrow nationalism. So the psalms miss their own truths when they call for revenge and destructiveness.

Those who use psalms these days recognize this tragic split. They red-line out the tragic and use that part of each psalm which is creative. They recognize that they cannot pray for anyone's ruin. Or else they shift the tragic realism of the psalms into a kind of myth, an allegory of the battle between spiritual forces in which no actual blood is spilled, no actual heads roll, rather, satanic forces are driven away much as in books V and VI of Milton's *Paradise Lost*. There is a certain amount of exhilaration in such uses of psalms. A certain catharsis. I am pointing out that the incompatibility between imagery of creation and imagery of destruction derives from the two imageries, not from consciousness developed outside them. If one stays outside these imageries, one can fail to see the incompatibility and use both sets side by side as though they are givens and made compatible because they are from God. I go back to the tradition of the psalmists here and say they too held suspect contradictions yoked together by the argument that God wills it. Somehow there was a sense even God had to make. The modern users of psalms have that same sense if they live the psalmists' imagery with any empathy. It may be that the traditions of sacred song have helped users of psalms to gloss over the imagery of violence. The beauty of the music became the source of spirituality, replacing the words. The soul was left with a sense of beauty, not a sense of horror. Or it may be that users of psalms put up with the tragic split because they accepted as a truth that the human mind could not grasp the good purposes of God in the revelation hidden under what seemed to be bad purposes. And there is a further appraisal of psalms which allows their use as wholes. They reveal fallen nature to fallen people, but in such way that fallen people know they can pray to God out of fallen nature. They need not be pure before they pray. What such an attitude does, I think, is create a fallen God to justify fallen nature. Then that God is asked to rage and storm and take revenge, to cause everlasting death. It is necessary to live and pray out of what one is. The best way, I think, is to sense there is a God of mercy who is also a God of truth, for the truth is as healing as mercy.

It may be that my process of translation skews the psalms to my own purposes as much as the use of psalms I have just described. I thought I had to approach the materials as a dramatist would. I have a great admiration for Aeschylus in his writing of the *Oresteia*, and for Sophocles in his writing of the *Theban Plays*, especially *Oedipus the King*. But most of all for Shakespeare in his writing of *Othello*, the ability to present so distinctly such contradictory characters as Iago and Desdemona, and such a frail warrior as Othello. The dramatic imagination seems to render to each character his or her due, and yet it enters fully into each character. I have said elsewhere that I think a lyric imagination would explode if it lent itself to expressing evil. Not that the lyric imagination is the one innocent in a guilty world. But it has to present itself. Not someone else. I wanted to render to each psalmist his due, and in that way not to skew in my direction what each said.

It was necessary to pick up the voice of each psalm. That meant I had to have a voice of my own, the translator's tool. That meant a match up if possible between the best I could do with dramatic, poetic language, and the best sense I could get of what a whole psalm meant. That involved consultation with Hebraists, with analyses, with commentaries. But it also meant a personal judgment about the nature of the voice in the psalm. For that I had to depend on my own poetic and theological sensibilities. There is the point where creativity entered the translation process. It is the most necessary part, the most risky, the most up for judgment.

The use of a dramatic imagination as a method of translation led me to notice the many different voices the tragic psalms contained, and to notice how they demanded distinctive presentation in all but a few instances. Even the recounting of common events by different psalmists became distinctive. That meant to me they should be hard to use by a group in the group's own voice, though used they were and are. People quote *Macbeth*, "out, out brief candle," and the phrase is good about the shortness of life. In context, however, it is a murderer speaking at the pitch of his despair. Though I found the various psalmists' voices tragic, I had to let them speak and to stand apart from the way they were used. The more I let them speak, the more I saw them missing their own truths, the more I felt pity and fear. I found myself caught up in their passions and I knew it could be but a short step before I would find myself made righteous as well by passion. I had to stay dramatic, not become lyric and a contradiction.

The seducing power of passion is very great, especially passions of righteousness, of anger, of revenge. It occurs often that passion then separates out from what causes it and becomes an ecstatic experience or an unmatched exhilaration. Warriors and lovers both know this. Translators do too if they give themselves fully to the emotions expressed in the texts. Even if translators stay within a dramatic imagination. It is then that translators can notice, as I think I did, that consciousness separates passion out to save itself the horror of knowing what it is doing if the passion is caused by destructive behavior or desire. It is as if consciousness simply cannot entertain destructivity except under the guise of procreativity. There is a further interpretation to be noted. Consciousness knows it cannot survive the passions of destructivity. I want to use an illustration here, though it may prove to be more of a distraction. I saw on television some years ago the American sergeant who served as the hangman for the Nazi war criminals at Nuremberg. The reason he appeared was that many years after doing his job he became profoundly disturbed in soul and could not at all understand why, since what he had done was sanctioned by every value he held. His life had become a torment and what tormented him was out of his reach. He was in therapy. The station that interviewed him was deeply interested in the man's problem, but as news only, so far as I could tell. I have no idea what happened after. The incident has become for me a metaphor for the effect of any killing on the one who does it, even though I know other hangmen may have died at peace. Consciousness has to transform the act into something it can live with. An example of what I am saying is this: eros does not derive from an experience of destructivity. It is a defense against the overwhelming truth of what one is doing or has done. It is an attempt to absorb death into life. If one does not know that, the temptation to accept erotic passion as a validation of destruction is very great. If one does know that, erotic passion becomes a warning to look at what one is doing and to whom. Eros that is constantly in mind of its cause is another matter. That sort tends to be truly creative, procreative. It stays relational. I have read aloud my version of Psalm 18 to small audiences. I have noticed a reaction of passion but one deeply troubled by the cause. I have read Psalm 104 from *Lyric Psalms* to people also. The passion is relational and not troubled, except over a few lines at the end.

It may be a credit to the many translations of psalms I have read that they try to soften the brutal feelings they must present. Psalm 18 has a warrior king say he loves his God. Love is scarcely the word for being taught by a divinity how to slaughter foes. Yet the word love is used and can be said in prayer by someone whom God has taught to care for the widow and the orphan and to welcome the stranger. The softening of the language of the texts shows that the religious soul wants to use the "word of God" for its prayer but also shows there is a point beyond which it cannot go. So what use would I suggest for these psalms in which I have tried not to soften the language?

I would say read them, hear them, in any translation, as one would read or hear Greek tragedy, with no sense of superiority, with every sense that given certain pressures one could become like the psalmists very quickly. But do not become them, do not make them into one's own voice. The effect I hope for will be the ability to see the psalms for themselves, to respect them for what they are, unique compositions mostly, which have their own character, however they came to be put together. The independence of psalm and reader/hearer will nurture a way of knowing in religion which deals with concrete, complex situations. One can appreciate the plight of the voice in Psalm 89 but also see how that psalmist's sense of God was bound to lead to bitter disappointment. One can understand the voice of the psalmist in Psalm 18, and also see what that savage self-preservation leads to. Or what the curses in Psalm 109 do to the one who curses. Above all one can see the stark difference between images of creativity and images of destructivity within the same psalm, from psalm to psalm, then in modern circumstances where there are frightening analogies in the holy wars, the holy seizures of land, the holy administrations of punishment, etc. If these psalms are approached as dramas they become part of a wide range of pieces that consciously or unconsciously mark out the human condition and teach it some hard lessons. The Aztecs had psalms. The Spaniards who conquered them allowed a few to be saved. And those psalms serve to intensify our sense of the tragic split in the Aztec's life, a nostalgia for permanent life on the one hand, a thirst for human sacrifice on the other—for religious reasons maybe, but that compounds the horror. The tragic psalms are also sobering things. That is their primary use, to sober us up to ourselves. Slim pickings it might seem. Homer can do as well.

The tragic psalms also sober us up to God. By the time we are through them we are longing for the creator God, and for the Suffering Servant of that God. We want the lyric sense, the truth sense, and we want the justice sense of that God as available in imagery as the destructive senses. It is not a question of ridding ourselves of imagery. Again, this might seem like slim pickings. Both Aeschylus and Sophocles can do as well. But I think the tragic psalms have the seeds of their own reversal. I mentioned this when I said the tragic psalmists had failed to see the truths of their own imagery. And it is doubly bad when we too fail to see the mercy forgotten, the universality forgotten. The Apollo of Aeschylus, the Apollo of Sophocles, are almost mindless to those two dramatists.

I would not use the tragic psalms, in any translation, for communal prayer. I would read them whole to communities for the two reasons I gave above. I would read them as dramatically as possible and let them create the effects of passion and unease. Selecting out lines is tantamount to writing new psalms. Whole psalms should be read. A certain fear comes over me when I hear the complete psalter referred to as the prayer of the church. I fear the sword dance and ecstatic vengeance of Psalm 149. I fear the brain bashing of Psalm 137, the torture called for in Psalm 120, the slaughter left and right in Psalm 118, the curses of Psalm 109, whomever they belong to. I even fear the self-righteousness of beautiful 139. And on down to Psalm 2 where God, if angered, makes people perish and quickly. Maybe some psalms are the prayer of the church. Maybe others are its cross.

I would use the tragic psalms as a schooling in intensity, intensity of relationship with God, the way Elie Wiesel uses them, as reasons to transform a tradition and create a new colloquy. Psalm 89 once again provides an example, though the psalmist still wants God to be what God once was, Israel's unquestioning defender. Wiesel wants God to be compassionate enough to cry out against the slaughter of innocent victims. And he wants human beings to do the same. There are new psalmists all around carrying on the intensity of relationship in new voices. Maybe these new voices would involve us in new tragedies. I have no guarantee they won't. But I think the church has had to write its own psalms, and write them generation after generation, though not calling them such. I would give preponderance to that tradition. When I pray in the name of Jesus, I have to pray for creation, or re-creation, or transformation, or straight-out mercy, or straight-out healing, or for forgiveness, or for union, or for companionship, or for straight-out love. I find it impossible to curse in the name of Jesus, even a fig tree, even those who destroy the souls of children, or those who twist religion into an instrument of personal power. I do pray for the pressure of the truth on such people and pray that the pressure be everlasting if need be, and that God be the truth that is the pressure.

ORATORIO

JONAH: AN ORATORIO

Narrator:
There was a day when evil
arrived in God, like the day
the moon nearly blocked the sun
for just a time and made it
wear a ring of beads on fire,
a collar around its neck
for just a time, then left it,
the voices of the killers
and killed a collar on God.

King of Ninevites:
I have power to kill. I use it
to make all life mine and ecstatic,
against the gods of others who think
I am just firewood for their ovens.
I am the fire. I make gold of flesh,
I fatten the night with gold faces,
and the oven, and the glowing coals,
the open throat of a tongueless grave.
I feed daylight gold from wrecked cities
until it vomits like a glutton.
I am not god, but each god I know
clears the earth for his people this way.
Even with me. But I will end up
as I want, not wood for some god's fire.

People of Israel:
God, do to them what they did to us.
Let them know terror before they die,
but let them die, smashed against the rocks
as our babies' heads, out on the roads
as our women where carrion birds ate
their beautiful eyes as so much dung.
We are helpless. You are not. You can
lay fire on their heads and wind and rain
as You once did conquering chaos
and the promised land You cleared for us
of vicious gods, made it fat with crops

and thick with honey for us alone,
who now beg of You from the mouth of death
to cause our killers terror to match!

Narrator:
That day God spoke to Jonah
out of anger, out of grief!

God:
You see those who cross my face
are the same ones who cross yours
and leave you on fire with rage.
Take that rage to them and say:
FORTY DAYS AND YOU ARE DEAD!
As dead as this sun and moon!

Narrator:
Jonah said nothing to God.
Then God saw that Jonah knew
and chose to make them perish.
For he alone could hear God,
he alone could make God heard.
He went to a port and took
a ship west out of the world
where he was the voice of God,
a cargo ship, a small crew
who knew nothing of prophets
or God's fire concealed in them.
So the squall that tore their sail
and the waves that crashed on board,
the clouds that grabbed for their hair
were someone not after them
and they fought the storm with fear.

Sailors:
That wail is not wind, it's death,
or the dead, it's the dead out
of death, the sea, the clouds, they
search us for someone they know.

Wind:
I am not you.
I want no more.
It is nothing to me
the death you want.

Water:
I want your life.
I cannot take it.
I would make my own
the death you want.

Clouds:
I want your words.
Not as they are now.
They would make of me
the death you want.

Sailors:
We are not the one they know
who can give them back their peace.
Lighten this ship! Lighten ship!

Narrator:
Jonah knew. He went below
frozen with rage, deaf and dumb
to the broaching ship and crew
and slept the sleep of the dead,
but they would not let him be.

Captain:
Face this storm with us. Get up!
Face your god too with our fate!
Someone somewhere can stop this!

Sailors:
The cause is on board this ship.
One of us has crossed a god
who flails at us like terror!
You, no! You, no! You, no! You,
Jonah! The short draw is yours!
Who sent this storm to get you?
What do the dead of the world
want from you, some vengeance?
Some mercy? Whose god is yours?
Whose blood is yours? Whose country?
If we know we may survive!

Jonah:
A Jew's blood, a Jew's God, from
the land of God, from the sky,
from the living sea of God

who has put a word in me
and damned if I will say it!

Sailors:
And damned for us if you don't!
This storm will last. Your God
will get you and us with you.
We are upside down. The clouds,
the waves are swapping places.
How are we to keep you safe?

Jonah:
You are not to. You take me,
you throw me into that sea
and that sea will stop, that wind
will stop. I know who it is.
The storm will die if I do.

Narrator:
Jonah knew. But he was God
to them. He had a sacred life.
They fought for him against God.
They rowed for land with one back.
They would not take any life
for fear of losing their own
if the God should be sorry
when Jonah was half way down
and drown them too in anger.
But the storm grew more deadly
so they said to Jonah's God:

Sailors:
Take him, not us! Blame yourself,
not us! You want it this way,
not us! We will pitch him out!
Jonah, go! God help you! Us!
Row this thing, row this damn thing!
O God, the sea is down flat!
The wind is gone out of it!
The clouds are flat like a hand!
Take what we have for yourself!
We will take what you will give!

Narrator:
Jonah knew the sea monster

who ate him alive was God
and he would stay mute in God
day and night until he said
yes, just as God would stay mute
in him until God said no!
He said yes. But it was no,
after three days, three nights shut.
He spoke the way people speak
to God when God afflicts them:

Jonah:
My soul is lost but you can hear me
beg you to save it from this hellmouth
in deep water where you have put me
to watch your waves live beyond my reach.
I am not yours, a stranger to you,
not allowed to see your holy face.
This is to drown, Lord, this is death deep
at the roots of you, in the marshes,
under mountains, head tangled in reeds
at the roots of you, this is to drown,
to reach bottom, to have its doors shut
me away from you and not open,
except to you if you take my soul
from this deadly place into your life.
If I lose hope, I know you never do.
My despair can touch your sacred face,
not a clay god's who would split my soul
from you with nothing but empty looks.
I will have you to thank, you the one
to find my soul, you the only one.

Narrator:
Jonah knew the sea monster
who spat him ashore was God.
For the second time God said:

God:
Get up, walk their city streets.
Tell the people who killed yours
what I told you I will do.
For you alone can hear me,
you alone can make me heard.
They are dead unless they change.

210

Narrator:

Jonah took the rage of God
to those who killed his people
with the hope they would not hear.
They were a mob in number.
They were a mob in riches.
Their city took days to walk.
Its power was low thunder.
To it Jonah spoke for God:

Jonah:

FORTY DAYS AND YOU ARE DEAD!

Narrator:

It took one day to reach them.
They knew which God Jonah meant
and how they could stay alive.
So they ate nothing, they drank
nothing, they wore beggars' clothes.
They made everyone obey.
The King took their choice as his:

King:

I put aside my power to kill,
to wrap my evil in ruling cloth.
With the ashes of my life, the rags
of flesh left me, I submit to God.
We are agreed: We will thirst for life,
We will starve for life. We will be bare
of life, bone bare, man, woman, child, beast.
We will moan for life as cattle moan
in birth or death. We will know the grief
we made others know and stop it there,
drop our hands, drop our violence,
raise our hands, raise our hands up empty
as our victims. God may see us then,
not through killing rage but pity's eyes.

Narrator:

God saw them give up evil.
God gave up evil toward them.
But Jonah gave up nothing
of his rage for punishment.
He still begged God to kill them,
but the heart was out of him.

Jonah:

You will not keep to your word I said
to you back home when you first got me.
You see why I went as far away
from you as I could in a hurry!
I know you are soft, quick to listen,
quick to forgive, slow to get angry,
never give up, not on those you love,
not on those you hate. You harm no one!
I am not you! I want your word to
kill them or my life is worth nothing.
You have to choose again. It is death
for me this way, a death I welcome!

God:

Your anger is death!

Narrator:

Jonah left God. He went east
to sit above the city
on a seat he made of rocks
to watch the city perish
and to give himself some shade.
God took a day to grow him
a plant to cover his head,
to protect him from sunstroke.
He took it as merciful
as he stared at the city.

Plant:

I want your life.
I cannot have it.
I cast a shadow
too small for you.

Narrator:

God took one night to wither
the plant on him with a worm.
He was bare of shade by dawn.

Plant:

I want your death.
I cannot bring it.
I have made the risk
too large for you.

Narrator:
The sun rose behind his back,
laid a desert wind on him,
then beat down upon his head.
He had nothing left to breathe.
He took it as merciless
while he stared at the city
to watch if it should perish.

Jonah:
If nothing happens to it
I am better off to die
the way you killed that plant.

God:
You thought that was merciless
and the shade was merciful!
You thought the sun merciless
but your own death merciful
if that city does not die!
Where has your anger brought you?

Jonah:
It has brought me to the truth!

God:
To pity what I do to
a plant and not a people?
A plant I grew in one night
and caused to die the next?

Jonah:
The shade plant was innocent!

God:
And not pity a people,
a people without number
who live in ignorance of
right and wrong like animals?

Jonah:
They had to admit their guilt!

God:
Is that not the death you want?

Narrator:
That day Jonah walked away

from God but God pursued him,
a silent moon, silent sun,
but when some evil crossed them,
the same quarrel erupted
like a ring of beads on fire,
a collar around their necks:

Jonah:
The shade plant is innocent!

God:
Is it not the death you want?

ORATORIO: JONAH

Narrator:
Have you a question to ask
the sacred books of life?

Voice:
What will happen to my life
if I want vengeance from God
on those who kill my people?

Narrator:
You must tell me why you ask.

Voice:
It is now like living death.

Narrator:
I will ask the sacred books.
Spirit of truth, let my life
be one with this living death.
Then lead me to a scripture
where I will see myself
what will happen to me there.
(silence)
JONAH THE PROPHET AND GOD
(silence)

God:
Is it not the death you want?

                              END

(or)
God:
Is it not the death you want?

Narrator:
The living death of Jonah
is the living death of God.
That is what this scripture says.
It will happen to your soul.

                              END

Sound in Sequence:

  *unison = same note, different timbres.
  *split   = different notes, different timbres.
  *echo   = one voice bleeding into and out of many voices.

Narrator:	contralto-baritone duet/unison
Nineveh:	baritone-mixed chorus/echo
Israel:	bass-mixed chorus/echo
Narrator:	contralto-baritone duet/split
God:	tenor-mezzo duet/split
Narrator:	contralto-baritone/split
Sailors:	bass-baritone-tenor-male chorus/echo
Wind:	soprano-female chorus/echo
Water:	soprano-female chorus/echo
Clouds:	soprano-female chorus/echo
Sailors:	bass-baritone-tenor-male chorus/echo
Narrator:	contralto-baritone duet/split
Captain:	bass-male chorus/echo
Sailors:	bass-baritone-tenor-male chorus/echo
Jonah:	bass/unaccompanied
Sailors:	bass-baritone-tenor-male chorus/echo
Jonah:	bass/unaccompanied
Narrator:	contralto-baritone duet/split
Sailors:	bass-baritone-tenor-male chorus/echo
Narrator:	contralto-baritone duet/split
Jonah:	bass-mixed chorus/echo
Narrator:	contralto-baritone duet/split
God:	tenor-mezzo duet/split
Narrator:	contralto-baritone duet/split
Jonah:	bass/unaccompanied
Narrator:	contralto-baritone/unison
King:	baritone-mixed chorus/echo to unison
Narrator:	contralto-baritone duet/unison
Jonah:	bass/unaccompanied
God:	tenor-mezzo/unison
Narrator:	contralto-baritone duet/unison
Plant:	mezzo-female chorus/echo to unison
Narrator:	contralto-baritone duet/unison
Plant:	mezzo-female chorus/echo to unison
Narrator:	contralto-baritone duet/unison
Jonah:	bass/unaccompanied
God:	tenor-mezzo duet/unison

216

Jonah:	bass/unaccompanied
God:	tenor-mezzo duet/unison
Jonah:	bass/unaccompanied
God:	tenor-mezzo duet/unison
Jonah:	bass/unaccompanied
God:	tenor-mezzo duet/unison
Narrator:	contralto-baritone duet/unison
Jonah:	bass/unaccompanied
God:	tenor-mezzo duet/unison

The Book of Jonah is the vantage point from which to view the tragic psalms. That is why it is included in a volume with them. Mercy is above all the works of God toward Israel. And therefore toward the whole of creation. So if Israel wants mercy for itself, it must want mercy for everyone else. That truth would stagger anyone who happens to survive a slaughter like the destruction of Jerusalem. It goes counter to the most natural prayer in the world. Read psalms 79, 137, 139, 140, 141 for some sense of what a ruined soul would pray. See that soul as a Jonah type. Then read the Book of Jonah and recognize its major insight: if you pray vengeance on your enemies, you will lose the last thing left you, your God. Jonah is ready to do that rather than preach repentance to the Ninevites. He knows that God responds to pleas for mercy with mercy. And he does not want that to happen. The small book teaches more than the failure of prophecy in Israel at that time after the return from Babylon, though the story is set some centuries earlier. It teaches that if Israel loses the sense of God as mercy, it does not know God anymore, and the conquest of its soul is complete.

That insight is the basis for all my decisions about making an Oratorio from the Book of Jonah. The additions I have made at the beginning are required in order that an audience can grasp the problem. The book itself starts *in medias res*, for an original audience that was quite aware of the rubble of Israel all around it and the reason why. A modern audience has to be set down in that rubble, but in such way that it becomes aware of rubble of its own kind and hence of the modern problem of God and of the mercy of God. The additions I have made at the end are also required if a hearer is to grasp the open ended nature of the original story. It seems to stop abruptly, inconclusively. What it really does is float the question free of itself like a balloon out over a crowd to be passed along upstretched hands who knows where. The material between the added beginning and end has been reduced to simple lines and to dramatic voices for the one purpose of making it easier to be grasped as heard. I have done something new by making the voices of nature express an insight not present directly in the original story. And I have used an image I found in nature as a modern way of grasping an ancient story. The image comes from what is called an anular eclipse of the sun by the moon. The sun itself is blocked but not the fires that shoot out from it. What one sees is a black sphere wearing a necklace of fire. The image of Jonah on God.

The reasons for using the image come from what the story itself implies. Jonah and his tradition are the only ones who know of a merciful God. They have benefitted from that mercy many times. And they are the only ones who can preach that mercy convincingly to the world. So by paradox, God's voice depends upon Jonah's voice and Jonah knows this. That is why he flees, taking the voice of God with him. That is why God pursues him, to regain a voice. Jonah has God reduced almost to a black hole. But not quite.

Jonah and his tradition also know that the very worst human reality is reachable by the very best human reality, and even by the very best divine reality. Torment doesn't work. Psalm 106 shows this. And despair about human nature does not work either. Those who despair have to leave this world. They have to leave all hope of sense behind, including whatever sense revenge makes. Creation has to be dropped. Every cultural and religious system must be based on a universalism. That often leads to the tragedy of conquest, if universalism is misunderstood to mean there is no truth but the one truth rather than that everyone can understand this truth if he or she wants to. The hope of change in a criminal is the only thing that brings a cultural or religious system into use. The moon eclipsing the sun takes away the light of both, though some light escapes because there are mountains and valleys to the moon which keep it from being a perfect shield.

Jonah and his tradition also know they are called to absorb evil and transform it into the very force that saves the evildoer. It is not that they are to seek out evil, not to live with prudence about life. It is that they have been given a vision of what God would do about evil in the Suffering Servant songs of Isaiah when that evil was inflicted on that Servant. Israel. An impossible difference between one people and other peoples. In the history of religions, however, there are examples of people coming to nearly the same insight though from different senses of God. I refer to the Bodhisattva types in later Buddhism, to the Quetzalcoatl figures in meso-America before the Spaniards or Aztecs, and to the savior ancestor in Dogon mythology. What an awful position for Servant Israel to be put in, a position of having to be God without the means of God or the invulnerability of God in terms of flesh and blood. It is at this moment that Israel could feel that God could not do what God asked. Therefore Israel could not do it. But that led to thoughts which would make God disappear as God, and Israel as the beneficiary of God's truth and beauty. It is at that point that Israel knew the price was one of losing God if it lost its soul. Then if either of them lost their sense of mercy, they both were finished. There would not even be a necklace of fire to mark where the two lost out. Jonah is willing to lose God for everyone in order to have enemies pay for their crimes.

There may be something in Jonah and Jonah's tradition that goes beyond the Suffering Servant solution to what to do about evil. In the Book of Job, the last chapters, God speaking to Job out of the whirlwind, there may be more than God avoiding Job's question about why the innocent suffer by flooding Job with how ignorant he is of the mighty scale of God's work and the small scale of Job's or anyone's suffering. There is another insight possible into the same sequence of chapters. God is showing how evil, how innocent suffering, are absorbed by God. That means God undergoes everything experientially. So divinity is not out of reach of suffering. And its one way of being is to hold all things together and to suffuse them with beauty or creative force over a long period of time. It is that recognition which causes Job, who would not speak untruth for anyone, to admit of God that God is the ultimate innocent sufferer. Job is not erased by this. He belongs to a largeness he never thought existed. In the imagery of eclipse, the sun does absorb the moon without the moon ceasing to be. The beauty of the scene is fearsome. Then light returns to its separate beauties.

Jonah and his tradition also knew that life could come to a devastated land, a land associated with evil, desert places where cities of sin may once have been. All it took was rain, a storm that crossed the mountains, to make the deserts bloom. Nature was a metaphor for the instruments of God, though in the psalm tradition there was still imagery of forces of nature inhabited by lesser gods subordinated to the one God. When I come to forces of nature in the Oratorio, I add an element which may not be there. I know from Genesis that each thing is created good. Therefore each thing has its own integrity. What I give to the voices of nature is almost a complaint of nature at being used by God as an instrument to force some sense on Jonah. The wind, the water, the clouds say don't force us to be torments for any reason. I use feminine voices because the feminine is the most forced reality I know. It is as if God and Jonah both need a lesson about the true nature of creation. The voice of the plant is an especially important one. It would influence Jonah with its own way of being. That it should be made to grow in order to shade Jonah, then made to die in order to strip Jonah, then made into a comparison so that the worth of people is made so much the greater relative to its own worth is violence pure and simple. If the plant followed its own laws of growth in an impossible place, and the gift of itself in an impossible place, then its death there, it could have taught Jonah an equal lesson. Life has consequences built into it. The truth of something does not perish with the thing. Someone must know. I am making a plea to religious imagination not to assume divine control over what imagery means, over the things that imagery is based on. I appreciate what Susan Sontag has said about illness as metaphor. Someone who has cancer is innocently cancerous unless they have deliberately incurred it, an almost unthinkable exception. To call sin a cancer is a risky metaphor. It misses the nature of both sin and disease. So, while the forces of nature in the Oratorio do God's bidding, and while Jonah in the story recognizes what God is using on him, those forces complain, and it is the complaint of creation against misuse by the religious imagination. If nature is allowed to be metaphorical, then imagination can make multiple uses of the same experience of nature and the natural form is left to be itself. I have used the example of an anular eclipse to make a synthesis of the material in the Oratorio. That eclipse is first of all a thing of great beauty. Then it is an image of evil concealing good. Then it is an example of innocent suffering concealing the compassion of God. Then it is an example of the compassion of God absorbing all suffering, innocent and guilty alike. The last use of the image will be to show the constant willingness of God when eclipsed to seek the conversion of those who sin, not their damnation. Meantime I hope I never forget the beauty of that natural phenomenon, the anular eclipse of the sun. It may be that all this is suggested to me by the last chapters of Job where creation is allowed its own voice. And also by the author of Jonah. The elements that were manipulated had no effect on Jonah except to have him obey grudgingly, to preach a message he regretted preaching more after the message succeeded. He even seizes on the good argument that things are not to be manipulated, i.e., the plant, to imply that innocence requires revenge if it is to maintain itself and its relationship with God. The Oratorio stops there and floats out on the hearer.

223

The psalms in this volume, when read in the light of the Book of Jonah, are truly tragic. They lose for their readers the basic sense that the mercy of God is indissolubly linked to the human voice testifying to that mercy. They lose for their readers the vocation to become expressions of that voice. The vocation must come from elsewhere. They lose for their readers the sense of the terrible price to be paid for that vocation. And in what terrible circumstances. They lose for their readers the example of those who have followed the vocation Jonah refused. We have to turn aside from these psalms to find the people who summon evil itself to change and who sometimes succeed. So the tragic psalms lose for their readers a sense of whole communities whose punishments can be strictly corrective and involve the hope that anyone can change under the influence of human wholeness. Thus they lose for their readers the chance to challenge the cynicism evil causes about itself. Maybe most of all they lose for their readers a hope that God is working toward the goal of absorbing evil in exactly the way the Suffering Servant was asked to absorb it, not toward the goal of taking in a remnant and tossing the rest away. The doctrine of approbation/reprobation has done enough harm to hope.

The reward for following the vocation offered to Jonah is relationship with someone who does the same, but on a cosmic scale. There seem to be no limits to that relationship. It goes beyond the paradisal land gift described in Psalm 23 and in many another lyric psalm. It is a Naomi-Ruth relationship. The punishment for not following the vocation is not exclusion from relationship. The voice of God pursues Jonah. This surely is a God who does not want the death of anyone. It seems to be a no-lose situation. But there is no happiness in Jonah's choice, the choice to die rather than be merciful. It is a situation of loss no one can measure. Yet there is still life, and God can appeal to life. Jonah's climate is the climate of Sheol which was abhorrent to many a psalmist. Sheol is lifeless life: "One day of life lived/with you is better/than a thousand days/of life without you./One day at your door/is better, O God,/than a thousand days/in the house of death."

There is a realism to the insight of the author of the Book of Jonah. People pay the price of revenge to retain relationship. People also pay the price of mercy. These latter are not so clearly seen for what they are. They seem to be simpletons or traitors. Yet their presence in evil times shows the difference

224

that makes evil visible. Otherwise everything is made from the same cloth. I am thinking of those people in the modern camps, concentration or gulag, who refused to become like their jailers. Not out of a sense of superiority. But to remember what it was to be human. For the jailer as well as for themselves. That is not exactly the same as mercy. But is the well of mercy.

At the end of the Oratorio, I have placed two verbal frames which could make the Jonah story usable for a storyteller. There is a type of Indian theater in which a single actor asks an audience to present some spiritual problem. The actor then prays for guidance to choose some story from sacred history which could respond to the problem raised. At the end of the telling, the actor links the fiction with the fact of the question. The actor plays all the parts.

I have also included a poetic description of the voicing I thought went with the text. The way those voices move with each other, away from each other, against each other, expresses almost more than the words the intensity of the problem of mercy. The description is added mainly for the composer. The voice of God is male and female at the beginning, but split, disunified, as it expresses its angry demand on Jonah. The violence of the earth is in a clash of male and female voices. The narrator is of male and female to show that the insight is present from the beginning in the storyteller's voice. The voice of nature is female alone. The voice of the sailors is male alone. But the two alonenesses indicate there can be wholeness that is not destructive to male and female apart. The sailors and nature are moved by a certain integrity. When the earth gives up its violence, the voice is a blend of male and female. Toward the end, the voice of God, whose mercy has succeeded with the Ninevites becomes a blend of male and female. Jonah remains throughout an unaccompanied bass. The voice that pursues him is a blend of male and female. I know that sung words escape most audiences unless they know the text beforehand. So I wanted to build the power of the story into sound alone, making the music fully capable of bearing the tension and resolution. Every expression we have can tell this story, mime, dance, stage design. The struggle over mercy is in everything we do. It surrounds us, in fact, the way music surrounds us. Something gets through blocked ears. Nothing through blocked eyes.

Francis Patrick Sullivan is a Jesuit priest. He has published three volumes of poetry, *Table Talk with the Recent God* (Paulist Press, 1974), *Spy Wednesday's Kind* (The Smith, 1979), and *Lyric Psalms: Half a Psalter* (The Pastoral Press, 1983). He teaches courses on aesthetics and theology at Boston College and at the Gregorian University, Rome. He received a MacDowell Colony residency in the summer of 1986 to complete work on *Tragic Psalms*. He is presently translating the short tracts of Bartolome de las Casas into English in preparation for the 1992 "discovery year" anniversary of the New World. He is working with a subcommittee of the International Commission on English in the Liturgy on the preparation of a new liturgical psalter.

Aileen Callahan is a member of the fine arts faculties of Boston College and Regis College. She received an M.F.A. in painting from Boston University and studied at the Escuela Nacional de Pintura y Escultura, Mexico (Lincoln Scholar two years), and Skowhegan School of Painting and Sculpture. Her murals and other works are in collections in the United States and Mexico.